Barnfield College Library

R08867

Pregnancy

Editor: Tracy Biram

Volume 394

independence
educational publishers

First published by Independence Educational Publishers

The Studio, High Green

Great Shelford

Cambridge CB22 5EG

England

© Independence 2021

Copyright

This book is sold subject to the condition that it shall not,
by way of trade or otherwise, be lent, resold, hired out or otherwise
circulated in any form of binding or cover other than that in which it
is published without the publisher's prior consent.

Photocopy licence

The material in this book is protected by copyright. However, the
purchaser is free to make multiple copies of particular articles for instructional
purposes for immediate use within the purchasing institution.
Making copies of the entire book is not permitted.

ISBN-13: 978 1 86168 852 1

Printed in Great Britain

Zenith Print Group

Contents

Introduction

Pregnancy is Volume 394 in the issues series. The aim of the series is to offer current, diverse information about important issues in our world, from a UK perspective.

ABOUT PREGNANCY

Understanding pregnancy and related complications and losses is important for everyone, not just for women. Staying healthy when pregnant and looking after your wellbeing and mental health are topics explored in this book. Also, we look at birth and beyond, and what happens when things don't go to plan.

OUR SOURCES

Titles in the **issues** series are designed to function as educational resource books, providing a balanced overview of a specific subject.

The information in our books is comprised of facts, articles and opinions from many different sources, including:

♦ Newspaper reports and opinion pieces

♦ Website factsheets

♦ Magazine and journal articles

♦ Statistics and surveys

♦ Government reports

♦ Literature from special interest groups.

A NOTE ON CRITICAL EVALUATION

Because the information reprinted here is from a number of different sources, readers should bear in mind the origin of the text and whether the source is likely to have a particular bias when presenting information (or when conducting their research). It is hoped that, as you read about the many aspects of the issues explored in this book, you will critically evaluate the information presented.

It is important that you decide whether you are being presented with facts or opinions. Does the writer give a biased or unbiased report? If an opinion is being expressed, do you agree with the writer? Is there potential bias to the 'facts' or statistics behind an article?

ASSIGNMENTS

In the back of this book, you will find a selection of assignments designed to help you engage with the articles you have been reading and to explore your own opinions. Some tasks will take longer than others and there is a mixture of design, writing and research-based activities that you can complete alone or in a group.

FURTHER RESEARCH

At the end of each article we have listed its source and a website that you can visit if you would like to conduct your own research. Please remember to critically evaluate any sources that you consult and consider whether the information you are viewing is accurate and unbiased.

Useful Websites

www.babycentre.co.uk

www.ectopic.org.uk

www.eufic.org

www.independent.co.uk

www.metro.co.uk

www.motherandbaby.co.uk

www.nhs.uk

www.sands.org.uk

www.theconversation.com

www.themummybubble.co.uk

www.tommys.org

www.topdoctors.co.uk

Fetal development timeline

The transformation from a tiny fertilised egg to a fully-formed baby is an incredible process.

When you're pregnant, it can be exciting and moving to think about what your baby's getting up to in there. From his first heartbeat to the day he's ready to enter the world, here are the major milestones your baby will reach while he's still in your womb (uterus).

Of course, every baby is different, so these timings are just a guideline.

First trimester

Three weeks

When egg meets sperm, the fertilised egg is known as a zygote. It travels from your fallopian tube down to your womb, where it will continue to grow. You probably won't know you're pregnant for a few weeks yet, though.

Did you know? At this early stage, your midwife will calculate your due date by working back to the first day of your last menstrual period.

Four weeks

The ball of cells has officially become an embryo and is about the size of a poppy seed. The early brain and spinal cord (neural tube) will develop, allowing your baby's organs to start forming. Early versions of the placenta and umbilical cord will start to work and begin to deliver nutrients and oxygen to your baby.

Five weeks

Your baby's body is only about the size of a sesame seed, and he still looks more like a tadpole than a human being. In the first of many growth spurts, his intestines will start to develop and his arms and legs begin to sprout.

Six weeks

Your baby's tiny heart begins to beat and pump blood at twice the rate of yours. At this stage, he's about the size of lentil, and facial features such as eyes and nostrils are beginning to form. His tiny arm and leg buds are more noticeable, and muscle and bone tissue is building up.

Eight weeks

By this point, your baby's embryonic tail is just about gone. His organs are beginning to work and tastebuds are forming on his tongue. He can even bend his hands at the wrist.

Nine weeks

Your baby's now starting to look more like a tiny human being, with ankles, fingers and toes. It's still too early to tell the sex, but the genitals are also beginning to form.

10 weeks

Your embryo is now officially a fetus, and he is able to move his new limbs. His vital organs, such as kidneys, intestines, brain and liver, are now fully functional. He's even starting to develop tiny fingernails and toenails.

11 weeks

Your baby is almost fully formed, though he's still only about the size of a fig. He's growing longer and stronger, and his bones are beginning to harden. He can hiccup, though it's still too soon for you to feel it.

12 weeks

Your baby's brain is developing, honing his new reflexes. He may even squirm around if you prod your belly, though you're unlikely to be able to feel it at this stage. Your baby can curl his fingers and toes, and his eyes and ears have almost moved to their final positions.

Second trimester

14 weeks

Your baby's eyebrows and hair are beginning to grow and his facial expressions are getting a workout. He may also have discovered thumb-sucking. Your baby's genitals have

Fetal development

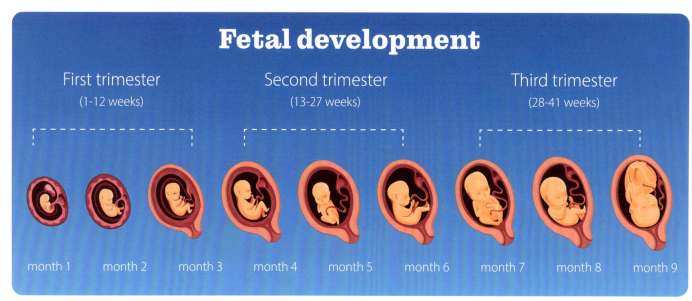

First trimester
(1-12 weeks)

Second trimester
(13-27 weeks)

Third trimester
(28-41 weeks)

month 1　month 2　month 3　month 4　month 5　month 6　month 7　month 8　month 9

developed to the point where it's sometimes possible to tell the sex from an ultrasound scan. However, you probably won't find out for sure just yet.

16 weeks

Your baby is now the size of an avocado and is getting ready for his next growth spurt. His little lungs have started to work, inhaling and exhaling amniotic fluid, and his circulatory system and urinary tract are both fully functional.

18 weeks

This is an exciting time, as your ultrasound scan in the next few weeks may show your baby kick, flex his fingers, and roll. You may also be able to find out your baby's sex.

19 weeks

Your baby's senses are developing as the parts of his brain responsible for taste, smell, hearing, sight and touch are becoming more refined. He's also started to grow a little hair on his head, and his kidneys are starting to make urine.

23 weeks

Your baby's hearing has now developed to the level that he may pick up a distorted version of your voice, your heartbeat and your tummy rumbles. You may start feeling your baby move at around this point, or even be able to see him squirming around.

Quick tip: You and your partner could try talking to your bump when you go to bed, or whenever your baby becomes more lively. The rhythm of your voice may be therapeutic, and your baby can hear your voice and other sounds from about 23 weeks.

24 weeks

Your baby's brain is growing rapidly, and his tastebuds are already fully formed. His lungs are developing quickly too, as they start to prepare for breathing air once he reaches the outside world.

Quick tip: About 90 per cent of women get stretch marks by this stage. Although there's no proven way to prevent them, you can always try to minimise their appearance by wearing a support bra. Rubbing oil or cream rich in vitamin E over your belly several times a day may also help, and will also help to relive itchy skin. A healthy diet rich in vitamin E, vitamin C, zinc and silica may help to keep your skin healthy.

27 weeks

Your baby's brain is certainly active at this point, and he sleeps and wakes at regular intervals, opening and closing his little eyes. He may also get regular bouts of hiccups, which can be quite an interesting sensation for you!

Third trimester

28 weeks

By now, your baby may be able to detect continuous bright lights outside your belly, and may even turn his head towards them. Fat layers are forming and his bones are nearly developed, though are still soft.

32 weeks

Your baby's skin is soft and smooth, and he may already have a full head of hair. If you're expecting a boy, his testicles will probably have moved down from his abdomen to his scrotum.

34 weeks

Your baby is getting plumper, developing layers of fat that will help regulate his temperature once he's born. If he's born prematurely the good news is that 99 per cent of babies born in week 34 can survive outside the womb, and most have no major problems.

37 weeks

Your baby is now considered full-term, and is likely to be fine if he's born now. However, he should ideally stay where he is for a few more weeks to give him a little extra chance to develop.

39 weeks

Your baby is due and he's fully ready for life in the big, wide world. Most doctors will wait for a couple of weeks before considering your baby to be overdue. Your baby's fingernails are long now and his skull bones are not yet fused, so he can move through the birth canal during labour.

The above information is reprinted with kind permission from BabyCentre
© BabyCentre 2021

www.babycentre.co.uk

26 weird early pregnancy symptoms

By Vicky Smith

How early can you really tell if you are pregnant? If you have been trying to conceive then you are probably finding that the wait from ovulation to positive pregnancy test feels like an absolute lifetime.

There's nothing quite so addictive when you want to fall pregnant than looking for symptoms everywhere.

Was that a twinge? Are my boobs bigger? Is this a period or implantation bleeding?

You could drive yourself a little crazy. Many women experience absolutely no early pregnancy symptoms at all. For some ladies, their body just doesn't react strongly to the pregnancy at first. They don't feel any different, so they just carry on, assuming their period will arrive on schedule in the next few days.

How soon can you tell if you are pregnant

The best way to confirm you are pregnant is with a positive pregnancy test!

There are various different types you can try, from simple strips that show up with a line to a digital display that shows 'pregnant' or 'not pregnant' to confirm levels of HCG. This is the hormone produced by the placenta after implantation has occurred.

Some tests can pick up levels of HCG five days before your expected period. So if your period is due on the 15th of the month, you could test positive on the 10th.

BUT everyone is different. A negative result five days, or even two days, before your period is due does not mean you are not pregnant. Many women find they need to wait until AFTER they have missed their period to get a positive result.

I tested negative twice with my first pregnancy. I thought I was definitely not pregnant. Then I felt so ill a couple of days before my period that I decided to do just one more test. Boom! I was pregnant, and I had thought I most definitely wasn't.

Early pregnancy symptoms

So if you just cannot wait for your period's due date to take a pregnancy test, how else can you tell if you are pregnant?

There are lots of symptoms to look out for! Unfortunately, they're not particularly pleasant, but if you are pregnant then it's all for a good cause!

You may not experience any of these symptoms at all, but some of these things could happen several days before you are able to get a positive pregnancy test result.

1. Light spotting

Implantation bleeding is what occurs when the fertilised egg attaches to the lining of your uterus.

Some ladies may mistake implantation bleeding for the start of their period. So how on earth can you tell the difference?

An implantation bleed will be much lighter, lasting only a few days. It may be pinkish in colour, or very dark brown to black. This type of bleeding will occur a few days before your period is due.

This does make it confusing, as you may assume you're definitely not pregnant this month when in fact all signs are good!

I had very heavy bleeding in the first eight weeks or so of both pregnancies. Because it lasted so long, it can't be attributed to implantation bleeding. Although it was investigated, no cause was ever found for my heavy bleeding but I have two very healthy children as a result.

So, implantation bleeding will only last for two to seven days. Possibly even less than this! You may just wipe and notice a

little pinkish tinged discharge, then think 'that's weird' and carry on with your day.

Timing is everything with implantation bleeding, so track your cycles and you will get a better idea of whether it's your period or a sign of early pregnancy. Implantation bleeding will typically occur around a week before your period is due.

What to do: If you suspect it could be implantation bleeding, use a sanitary pad and avoid using menstrual cups or tampons.

Keep track of the number of days it occurs and how heavy it is, which could give you a good indication of whether it is an actual period or implantation bleeding.

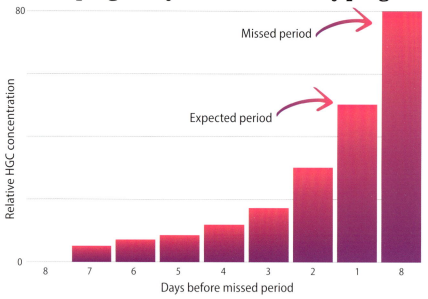

Rise of pregnancy hormone in early pregnancy

2. Swollen boobs

The hormonal changes that happen in your body as a result of pregnancy. As progesterone levels rise, your boobs can start to feel sore, sensitive or tender to the touch.

Bras that are usually comfy suddenly feel tight or like you want to get them off because they just don't feel right any more.

Your breasts will go through a LOT of changes during your pregnancy. This is because your body is gearing up for breastfeeding.

The fat layer in your breasts will thicken and your milk glands will get bigger. Plus the blood flow to your breasts will increase.

All of these things can begin to happen as early as 10 days before your missed period.

What to do: Stop wearing bras with underwear. Ditch them in exchange for some supportive sports bras or maternity bras.

At this stage its probably a little early to be investing in nursing gear, so stick to the sports bra option. Go for something with no padding or underwear to help keep you comfy.

3. Nipple changes

Nipples get bigger when you are pregnant! Nobody told me about this and I can remember one day during my pregnancy looking down and thinking 'woah, those used to be half the size!'

In the early days of pregnancy you may feel your nipples tingling and notice they are extra sensitive.

You won't see any growth in the first month of pregnancy, but watch out for strange feelings around this area ahead of your missed period.

4. Mood swings

You may think your PMSing when actually your haywire hormones are because of baby, not your usual pre-period moodiness.

You may find yourself quick to agitation, or crying at the silliest of things.

It's easy to miss mood swings, because at the time you won't necessarily think anything is wrong. You're just feeling

annoyed today! Or you just watched something on TV that made you feel particularly sad and tearful.

Your other half may well be the first to notice this one!

5. Weird food cravings

Did you used to absolutely adore tomatoes and now feel like just the thought of them will make you vomit?

Maybe you usually live for your morning coffee, but suddenly the idea of caffeine makes you want to flee as fast as you can from all coffee shops.

You may also start to crave things you usually don't eat very much, or things that you can usually just enjoy as the odd treat but not cannot stop thinking about.

If your cravings for food and drinks has changed, this is a sign you could be pregnant!

The change to your appetite for certain foods and sudden hunger for things you used to hate is down to hormones. It can also be because of changes to your senses, such as taste and smell.

What to do: Embrace the weirdness! If you want to eat a whole jar of pickles, then eat them. Try to keep up with a normal, balanced diet but satisfy your cravings (within reason) while you're at it.

Some pregnant ladies may experience a condition known is pica, which is where they crave odd non-foods during pregnancy. This may be things such as coal and rocks.

This is very rare and something to chat with your doctor about to get advice.

6. Elevated basal temperature

If you have been keeping tabs on your basal body temperature in order to track your cycles and pinpoint ovulation, then you'll be familiar with the term. If not you may be thinking, What?

Basal body temperature is the lowest body temperature attained during rest. You can estimate it by measuring your temperature immediately after waking up, before you even get out of bed.

Ovulation causes the basal temperature to increase by at least 0.2C (0.4F).

If you are pregnant, you may see a spike in a basal body temperature a week after ovulation.

Keeping track of your basal body temperature to track ovulation is also a good sign that you may have had sex on the right days to catch the egg.

This method is by no means an exact science and only really works if you have been keeping a really close eye on your basal body temperature for several weeks so you can see real patterns emerging.

7. Headaches

Ouch. This is one you could easily shrug off as just a headache. But, headaches are a common symptom of the first trimester.

This could be down to rising hormone levels and blood volume as your body is changing to nurture your baby.

Figuring out whether your headache is down to pregnancy or not can be tricky. If it feels as if it's in your sinuses then it's a potential sign of pregnancy, as nasal congestion is common in early pregnancy.

Migraine headaches are another common pregnancy symptom. These are definitely not fun! They can also cause nausea and vomiting.

Your early pregnancy headaches may also be down to ditching coffee, which means you could be suffering from withdrawal symptoms for the caffeine.

What can you do: If your headache is really bad, or a migraine, then get loads of rest and stick to a darkened room with no noise.

You should avoid aspirin and ibuprofen during pregnancy, so opt for paracetamol instead.

Drink plenty of fluids and try to avoid any triggers such as certain foods or smells that may set off a headache.

8. Dizziness

Feeling dizzy was one of the first symptoms that I felt during my first pregnancy. I can pinpoint the exact moment I felt a wave of dizziness hit me while I was sitting down at work one day.

The dizziness did not stop for several weeks. It wasn't bad enough that I was falling over, but it was a strange feeling!

Dizziness in pregnancy can happen due to the hormonal changes you go through as your body reacts to the pregnancy and increase in blood flow. This can cause the body to relax the walls of your blood vessels and cause blood pressure to fall.

What can you do: Sit down immediately! Try to stay still and take even, calm breaths.

Dizziness could also be down to you eating less due to hormones putting you off food. Try to eat something! Go for smaller, bland meals, such as bananas and toast. Eating little and often can help.

Remember to drink plenty of water and don't rush around too much.

Call your doctor if you feel so dizzy that you faint.

9. Gas

You may find yourself burping or farting more than often. This may be down to the increase of progesterone and oestrogen in your body, which causes the muscles in your body to relax. A common symptom of pregnancy is that your intestinal muscles relax, causing digestion to slow. This can then cause the gas to build up in your body.

What can you do: In the early weeks the increase in gas will be easier to control than when you are heavily pregnant and the gas has nowhere to go but out!

For now try to laugh it off if it happens and don't fight it too much. Stick to foods that don't make you as gassy, and avoid foods that are fried along with fizzy drinks.

10. Constipation

The pregnancy hormones cause your digestion to slow right down and this causes constipation.

It may be too early in your pregnancy for this to occur but many ladies in the first few weeks of their pregnancy report this condition.

What can you do: Eat foods that are high in fibre to help your bowels keep moving. This may include cereals, wholegrain rice and pasta plus fruits.

Prunes and prune juice can be great at helping you produce a bowel movement if you are getting desperate.

Remember to drink lots of water too.

11. Cramping

The cramps will not be as strong as normal period cramps. They may feel a lot lighter and may last just a day or two, but can also last for months. If they are mild they are nothing to worry about.

This is a sign of the normal physical changes happening to your womb as your baby implants and the placenta develops.

What can I do: Try natural remedies such as soaking in a warm bath, resting plenty, and holding a hot water bottle in the area to ease the discomfort.

12. Lower back pain

This can go hand in hand with the cramping. It's very natural, although it won't feel great if you're trying to carry on with your normal life!

What can I do: Try similar respite as described for cramping such as a warm bath. You could try adding some epsom salts to the water.

An elastic belly band may also provide some support and relief from the pain.

13. Bloating

Does your belly feel bloated, tight and uncomfortable? This is not because of an early baby bump! It's down to your digestive system slowing and the extra gas your system may be producing.

It can feel uncomfortable, and increase feelings of morning sickness, but it's normal.

14. Fatigue

There are a lot of changes going on in your body, so being tired is pretty expected!

During the first trimester is when most pregnant ladies report feeling especially tired as their body diverts energy to helping the placenta grow and nurturing the pregnancy.

Raised progesterone levels can also make your feel sleepy.

What can I do: Apart from resting up and drinking lots of fluids, there's not a whole lot you can do! Try to stay active with gentle exercise such as a daily walk. The fatigue will pass after the first trimester.

15. Nausea and vomiting

This is often called morning sickness which is extremely misleading as it can last all day and all night!

It is an unpleasant symptom of pregnancy, but for many women it clears up after the first trimester.

There is a more serious form of sickness in pregnancy called hyperemesis gravidarum. This condition is what plagued all three of the Duchess of Cambridge's pregnancies, and more recently comedian Amy Schumer's first pregnancy.

This involves a great deal of vomiting and can be serious as you may become dehydrated and struggle to get enough nutrients from food.

Vomiting and sickness could also indicate a UTI infection in the bladder, which is more common in pregnant ladies. Seek medical attention if you are worried.

What can I do: There are a lot of theories about what can help with morning sickness. But for some women nothing gets rid of it completely.

There are a few things you could try to ease your suffering:

♦ Many people swear by ginger as a way to combat morning sickness. Ginger biscuits are good option.

♦ A ginger peach green tea popsicle could help with your morning sickness

♦ Keep snacks next to your bedside. Many pregnant ladies find it helps to have something in their stomach before they even get out of bed. Have some dry crackers or ginger biscuits next to your bedside so that you can munch on one as soon as you wake up.

♦ Try an anti-nausea band. These apply pressure to your forearm and many pregnant ladies swear by them!

♦ Drink lots of fluids. Sipping little and often can prevent vomiting so keep a water bottle on you at all times.

♦ Eat smaller meals. Stick to smaller meals but eat more throughout the day. You may also find that eating cold food is better for your stomach than hot food.

♦ Eat plain food. Stick to foods high in carbs such as bread, rice, pasta and crackers.

16. Frequent trips to the toilet

During pregnancy your body will be producing more blood to facilitate changes to your body and nurture the growing baby.

This may lead to an increase in fluids in your body. As a result you may find yourself heading to the toilet more often.

What can I do about it?: This is a symptom that can last for the entire pregnancy, so get used to it, drink lots of fluids and always make sure you will be near a toilet wherever you go.

Whatever you do, don't stop drinking fluids as you need about 300ml additional fluids every day during pregnancy. Try to have a bottle of water with you at all times and take small sips rather than gulping down a huge glass all in one go.

17. Metallic taste

An odd, unpleasant or metallic taste in the mouth is quite a common symptom pregnant women experience.

The change is down to hormones, which can influence your senses and so cause your taste and smell to go haywire.

What can you do: Try rinsing your mouth with a salt water solution. Add a teaspoon of salt to 8 ounces of water and stir to dissolve. Swill this in your mouth for a minute then spit it out. This may only provide a temporary relief.

You could also eat sour flavours such as lemonade or foods marinated in vinegar such as pickles. This can help to break down the yucky taste in your mouth and produce lots of saliva to help to wash it away.

18. Stronger sense of smell

As part of the hormonal changes, you may find that you become averse to certain smells. You may also find you are more sensitive to smell, so walking by a restaurant might make your stomach churn as the scent is so strong.

If the intense smells are unpleasant then this can exacerbate pregnancy nausea too.

What can you do: Avoid cooking foods that cause a bad reaction. If you find certain places you used to visit smell so strongly you feel ill, avoid those triggers too.

19. Rumbling tummy and hunger

Have you noticed your tummy is particularly noisy, gurgling and spluttering when you normally don't have this issue at all?

This can be due to changes in your digestive system brought on by hormonal changes. You may also find your appetite increases and you are constantly hungry.

What can you do: Eat a balanced and healthy diet with three proper meals a day and healthy snacks in between. Drink plenty of fluids too.

20. White discharge

If you have been tracking your menstrual cycle to get pregnant, you will have noticed that your vaginal discharge changes throughout the month.

During early pregnancy you may notice a white or yellowish discharge. This could be down to hormonal changes happening or the closure of your cervix as your body changes to support the pregnancy.

This is nothing to worry about, but do contact your doctor if the discharge is a bright yellow or green and smells bad. This could be a sign of a yeast infection which is common in pregnancy.

21. Catching colds and flu

Got a runny nose? Sneezing constantly? Think it's just a cold? It could actually be caused by your pregnancy!

Many ladies report having a runny nose and feeling unwell during the early weeks. This is because pregnancy can lower your immunity and make you more vulnerable to coughs and colds.

What can you do: Get plenty of rest, which may mean taking time off work to recover, and make sure you drink plenty of fluids.

22. Heartburn

As pregnancy hormones cause your body's muscles to relax, this may cause the valve between your stomach and oesophagus to loosen.

Stomach acid can then leak upwards, causing heartburn.

What can you do about it: You can take heartburn medication such as Rennie during pregnancy. A glass of milk may also help.

Try to stay upright after eating for at least an hour to help keep your food down.

23. Stuffy nose

It's not a cold but your nose is constantly feeling stuffy! This is caused by hormonal changes during pregnancy.

It's difficult to tell the difference between a stuffy nose brought on by pregnancy and just a normal sinus issue. But if you are experiencing this with some of the other symptoms on the list then it could be a good sign you are pregnant.

What can you do: Sleep in a more upright position using pillows to prop you up and get comfortable. A warm shower before bed can also help as steam can relieve the congestion.

You could also try nasal drops which you can get from any pharmacy.

24. Shortness of breath

The increase in progesterone can cause you to breathe more often. This may feel like shortness of breath, but actually the hormone expands your lung capacity so that you can carry more oxygen around your body.

What can you do: Try to sit up straight and give your lungs room to slow down. It's also important to give yourself lots of rest and sit down if you do feel out of breath.

25. Excessive saliva

You may find yourself constantly swallowing back saliva. Excessive production of saliva is a normal part and can be blamed on hormones, nausea, or heartburn.

You may find that you produce so much extra saliva you actually have to spit it out. Yuck!

What can you do: There's not a whole lot you can do, but taking small and frequent sips of water may help. You could also try sucking on a hard sweet, as this will help you swallow the saliva without it being quite so unpleasant.

26. Spots

Were you expecting a pregnancy glow and ended up with a huge breakout of acne instead?

It's an annoying but common part of pregnancy and as your hormones change in the earliest weeks of pregnancy you could see it before a positive test.

The hormones associated with pregnancy may cause your skin to produce more oil which in turn causes spots.

What can you do: Manage your acne by washing your skin twice a day with a gentle cleanser. Avoid wearing too much makeup as this can irritate the blocked pores.

Important early pregnancy symptoms you should never ignore

Most doctors will tell you to stay away until you have had a positive pregnancy test. There's not much they can do for you until it's been confirmed you actually are pregnant!

But there are a few symptoms that may indicate something serious is going on. Do not ignore these warning signs if you think it could be pregnancy related.

Painful cramping

Cramping during early pregnancy should be extremely mild. It may include some lower back pain but it should not be on the same level as intense period pain cramps.

Pain that is very strong, and is concentrated to one side, should be assessed by a doctor. Pain isolated to one side could indicate an ectopic pregnancy and this needs to be treated immediately.

Very heavy bleeding

If the bleeding is very heavy, intense and lasts for more than a day, you should consult your doctor. It is particularly important that you do this when it is combined with severe pain as described above.

If you suspect you are pregnant, avoid using tampons or menstrual cups to deal with the bleeding as these could cause infection or additional issues.

Fainting

Dizziness is normal in early pregnancy, but if you are passing out, then you should see your doctor. This could be dangerous and may indicate your blood pressure has dropped too low and would benefit from some medication to help or investigation to assess the underlying cause.

I hope you found this list useful and gives you an idea of what to look out for in your early pregnancy. Remember, you may experience none of these in that frustrating two week wait.

The most reliable symptom of early pregnancy is a positive pregnancy test!

The above information is reprinted with kind permission from The Mummy Bubble.
© 2021 The Mummy Bubble

www.themummybubble.co.uk

10 steps to a healthy pregnancy

Taking good care of yourself during your pregnancy will give your growing baby the best start in life. Getting some exercise, eating well and keeping up with your antenatal appointments will all help you to have a healthy pregnancy. Learn more about the simple steps you can take.

1. See your doctor or midwife as soon as possible

As soon as you find out you're pregnant, get yourself registered for antenatal care. Register online with your local maternity service or make an appointment with your GP or a midwife at your local surgery or children's centre.

Organising your care early means you'll get good advice for a healthy pregnancy right from the start. You'll also have plenty of time to organise your diary for ultrasound scans and tests that you may need.

2. Eat well

Aim to eat a healthy, balanced diet whenever you can. This means having:

♦ At least five portions of fruit and vegetables daily. Fresh, frozen, canned, dried or juice all count. Choose fruit in its own juice or water rather than a sugary syrup and avoid vegetables tinned in salt water.

♦ Starchy foods (carbohydrates), such as potatoes, bread, pasta and rice. These should make up just over one third of all the food you eat. Choose wholegrain varieties rather than white, so you get plenty of fibre. Leave the skin on potatoes as it makes them more nutritious for you and your baby.

♦ Daily servings of protein, such as fish, lean meat, eggs, beans, nuts or pulses.

♦ Dairy foods, such as milk, cheese and yoghurt.

♦ Two portions of fish a week, at least one of which should be oily, such as salmon, sardines or mackerel.

Fish is full of protein, vitamin D, minerals and omega-3 fatty acids, which are important for the development of your baby's nervous system.

If you don't like fish, you can get omega-3 fatty acids from other foods, such as nuts, seeds, soya products and green leafy vegetables such as spinach and Brussels sprouts.

You don't need to eat for two when you're pregnant. In fact, you don't need any extra calories for the first six months of pregnancy.

In the last three months, you'll only need another 200 calories a day.

Stay well hydrated too. You need more water now that you're pregnant, to produce extra blood and amniotic fluid. Drinking plenty helps to prevent constipation and tiredness too.

Try to have about eight glasses of fluid each day. The healthiest way to stay hydrated is by drinking water, but there are other options to boost your daily fluid intake such as fruit teas and skimmed or semi-skimmed milk. Fresh fruit juice is packed with vitamin C but can be high in sugar, so drink in moderation.

3. Take a supplement

It's important for you and your growing baby to take folic acid and vitamin D supplements. You'll need to take these even if you eat a healthy and balanced diet.

Folic acid

You need to take folic acid while you're trying for a baby and for the first three months of pregnancy.

Taking folic acid reduces the risk of your baby developing a neural tube defect such as spina bifida. Some women need to take a higher dose of 5mg per day. You may be offered a higher dose if you have diabetes, or if you've had a previous pregnancy affected by a neural tube defect. Check with your GP or midwife what the best dose is for you.

Vitamin D

You also need a daily supplement of 10mcg of vitamin D throughout your pregnancy and beyond. Vitamin D helps your baby's bones and teeth to develop.

Other supplements

Most women get all the nutrients, vitamins and minerals they need from their diet and don't need to take other supplements. However, if you struggle to eat healthily, a pregnancy multivitamin may help you get the vitamins and minerals you need.

If your diet is good but you don't eat fish, you could take a fish oil supplement. Choose a supplement labelled omega-3 oil rather than fish liver oil. This is because fish liver oils, such as cod liver oil, may contain the retinol form of vitamin A, which may harm your unborn baby.

Talk to your GP, midwife or a pharmacist before taking supplements, other than the necessary folic acid or vitamin D. It's always better to have a balanced diet, if you can, rather than relying on multivitamins.

Multivitamins and supplements can be expensive. If you're on a low income, you may be able to get free pregnancy vitamin supplements under the government's healthy start scheme.

4. Be careful about food hygiene

Wash your hands before handling food, especially if you've just been to the toilet, changed a nappy, or handled a pet or other animal.

Thoroughly wash utensils, chopping boards and your hands after handling raw meat. Store raw foods separately from ready-to-eat foods. Food hygiene is especially important now you're pregnant.

There are also some foods it's safest not to eat in pregnancy. This is because they can harbour bacteria or parasites that pose a health risk for your baby.

Listeriosis is an infection caused by listeria bacteria. Although it's rare for pregnant women to be affected by it, it can have serious effects.

Listeriosis can lead to miscarriage, a baby being seriously ill after birth, or even being stillborn.

The following foods may contain listeria and should be avoided:

♦ pâté of any type

♦ unpasteurised milk

♦ undercooked ready meals

♦ soft, mould-ripened cheeses, such as brie

♦ blue-veined cheeses, such as roquefort

♦ smoked salmon

Salmonella bacteria can cause food poisoning. You can pick up a salmonella infection from eating:

♦ raw or undercooked meat

♦ raw shellfish

Eggs that have the British Lion red mark have a very low risk of carrying salmonella, so are safe to eat soft-boiled. Always cook eggs that don't have the red stamp until the white and yolk are solid.

Foods made from raw eggs, such as mayonnaise, are fine to eat if you know for sure that the eggs have been pasteurised or have the British Lion mark.

Toxoplasmosis is an infection caused by a parasite. It's rare, but it can cause miscarriage or affect your unborn baby, leading to blindness and neurological problems. You can cut your risk of catching it by:

♦ cooking meat and ready meals thoroughly and avoiding cold cured meats, such as salami

♦ washing fruit and vegetables well to remove soil or dirt

♦ wearing gloves when handling cat litter and garden soil

5. Exercise regularly

Regular exercise has many benefits for you, and therefore your baby.

Doing gentle exercise:

♦ Helps you to cope with changes to your posture and strains on your joints during pregnancy.

♦ Helps you to stay a healthy weight, although it's normal to put on some weight during pregnancy.

♦ Helps to protect you against pregnancy complications, such as high blood pressure and gestational diabetes.

♦ Increases your chance of a straightforward labour and birth.

♦ Makes it easier for you to get back into shape after your baby is born.

♦ Boosts your mood if you're feeling low.

Good exercises for pregnancy include:

♦ brisk walking

♦ swimming

♦ aquanatal classes

♦ yoga

♦ Pilates

Always let your exercise teacher know that you're pregnant or, ideally, choose classes tailored for pregnancy.

If you play sport, you can continue as long as it feels comfortable for you. However, if your particular sport carries a risk of falls or knocks, or extra stress on your joints, it's best to stop. Talk to your midwife or GP if you're unsure.

6. Begin doing pelvic floor exercises

Your pelvic floor is a wide sling of muscles at the base of your pelvis. These muscles support your bladder, vagina and back passage. They may feel weaker than usual in pregnancy because of the extra pressure on them. Pregnancy hormones can also cause your pelvic floor muscles to soften and slacken slightly.

Weak pelvic floor muscles can increase the risk of developing stress incontinence. This is when you leak wee when you sneeze, laugh or exercise.

You can strengthen your muscles by doing pelvic floor exercises, or Kegels, regularly throughout your pregnancy. You'll feel the benefit if you can build up to 10 long squeezes of 10 seconds, followed by 10 short squeezes, three times a day.

7. Cut out alcohol

Any alcohol you drink rapidly reaches your baby via your bloodstream and the placenta.

There is no safe level of alcohol to drink when you are pregnant and the more you drink the greater the risk of harm to your baby. That's why it's recommended that you cut out alcohol completely while you're expecting.

It's particularly important to avoid too much alcohol during the first trimester and the third trimester.

In the first trimester, drinking alcohol can damage your baby's development and can increase your risk of miscarriage, while in the third trimester it can affect your baby's brain. Other pregnancy complications linked with alcohol include preterm birth and stillbirth.

Drinking heavily or binge drinking during pregnancy is especially dangerous for your baby.

Mums-to-be who drink heavily on a regular basis are more likely to give birth to a baby with fetal alcohol spectrum disorders (FASD). These are problems ranging from learning and behavioural difficulties to more serious birth defects.

8. Cut back on caffeine

Too much caffeine may increase your risk of miscarriage and stillbirth late in pregnancy. Caffeine is in coffee, tea, cola, chocolate and energy drinks.

It may also contribute to your risk of having a low-birth-weight baby or a premature birth.

Current health guidelines recommend that you limit your caffeine intake during pregnancy to 200mg a day. That's the equivalent of two mugs of instant coffee.

As with alcohol, you may prefer to cut out caffeine altogether, particularly in the first trimester. Decaffeinated tea and coffee and fruit teas are all safe alternatives.

9. Stop smoking

Smoking during pregnancy can cause serious health problems for you and your baby.

Smoking increases your risk of:

♦ Miscarriage

♦ Ectopic pregnancy, where the fertilised egg implants outside the womb, usually in one of the fallopian tubes.

♦ Placental abruption, where the placenta comes away from the womb wall before your baby is born.

Smoking also increases your baby's risk of:

♦ premature birth

♦ low birth weight

♦ stillbirth

♦ sudden infant death syndrome (SIDS) or "cot death"

If you smoke, it's best to stop, for your own health and that of your baby. The sooner you stop smoking, the better, but it's never too late.

Ask your GP or midwife to help you with ways to stop. You can also call the confidential NHS Smokefree National helpline on 0300 123 1044 or visit NHS Better Health.

10. Get some rest

The fatigue you feel in the first few months is due to high levels of pregnancy hormones circulating in your body.

Later on, it's more likely to be because you're getting up in the night to go to the loo or not being able to get comfortable in bed.

Try to get in the habit of going to sleep on your side. By the third trimester, sleeping on your side reduces the risk of stillbirth compared to sleeping on your back.

If your sleep is disturbed at night, try to take a quick nap in the middle of the day or go to bed early to catch up. If that's impossible, at least put your feet up and relax for half an hour.

If aches and pains are disturbing your sleep, lying on your side with your knees bent and a firm cushion between them may help. Placing a wedge-shaped pillow under your bump may ease the strain on your back.

Exercise may also give you some relief from backache. It can help you have better quality sleep too. It's best to avoid exercising too close to bedtime, so try to fit it in earlier in the day, if you can.

To unwind before going to bed, or to get back to sleep during the night, try a relaxation technique, such as:

♦ yoga

♦ stretching

♦ deep breathing

♦ visualisation

♦ massage

A warm bath or reading a book in the evening may also help you drop off more easily.

The above information is reprinted with kind permission from BabyCentre.
© BabyCentre 2021

www.babycentre.co.uk

Healthy pregnancy: what foods to eat when pregnant

Abalanced and nutritious diet is essential for good health, and even more so during pregnancy, as eating well will give you most of the nutrients that you and your baby need. A healthy diet and lifestyle will also help ensure a healthy weight gain, ensure you get the key vitamins and minerals you need, and reduce your risk of pregnancy complications.

What should I eat for a healthy pregnancy diet?

Most European countries have their own food-based dietary guidelines (FBDGs), often represented as a food pyramid or food plate. Following the guidelines developed by your own country can help you get the nutrition you need during pregnancy for you and your baby.

Just like the general dietary guidelines, during pregnancy you are advised to eat a variety of foods from each food group represented within the guidelines every day, including grains and starches, fruits and vegetables, proteins, dairy foods or plant-based alternatives, and fats and oils.

Here are some general principles to help you stick to a healthy diet during pregnancy:

Meeting your energy needs

Energy needs increase throughout pregnancy, but it is a myth that you need to "eat for two". Non-pregnant women need on average around 2,000 kcal (calories) per day. During pregnancy, this increases by:

♦ +70 kcal/day during the first semester – equivalent to one additional slice of whole grain bread

♦ +260 kcal/day during the second semester – equivalent to one added bowl of fruit and yoghurt

♦ +500 kcal/day during the third semester – equivalent to one extra medium-sized meal

Grains and starches, preferably whole grain

Grains, especially whole grains, and starches are important during pregnancy because they provide you with carbohydrates, which our bodies use for energy, and fibre, minerals and vitamins. Try to include wholegrains, such as whole wheat pasta, brown rice, oats or other starchy foods like potatoes at every main meal.

Eat plenty of fruits and vegetables

Fruits and vegetables are packed full of vitamins and minerals important for you and your growing baby. They are also rich in fibre, which, when consumed with plenty of fluids, can help to prevent constipation. Aim for at least five portions of around 80 g every day – around 400 g per day in total.

What makes a portion of fruit & veg?

berries 1 handful	**small fruits** 2 pieces	**medium fruits** 1 piece	**large fruits** 1 slice
root vegetables 1 fist	**peas or sweetcorn** 3 heaped teaspoons	**leafy salad** 2 handfuls	

processed fruit & veg are also good choices

frozen same as fresh or 80g	**canned** same as fresh or 80g	**dried** 1 heaped teaspoon or 30g	**smoothie/juice** (max. once a day) 1 glass (150ml)

Source: eufic

Include more fibre in your diet

Choose wholegrain varieties

Keep the skins on potatoes

portion sizes

2 handfuls of wholegrain pasta

2 slices of wholegrain bread

1 fist-sized potato

Source: eufic

Nutrient highlight: Vitamin A

Vitamin A is essential for the development and functioning of your baby's skin, eyes, lungs and digestive system. Vitamin A is found in foods such as liver, whole milk, and cheese. Our bodies can also make vitamin A by converting compounds known as carotenoids (such as beta-carotene) found in many fruits and vegetables like carrots, green leafy vegetables and oranges.

Although vitamin A is important during pregnancy, too much can be harmful to your developing baby. Therefore, during pregnancy or when trying to conceive you should avoid supplements containing vitamin A unless advised by a health professional. Liver and liver products are also best avoided when pregnant as they contain high amounts of vitamin A. See Healthy pregnancy: foods to avoid when pregnant.

Choose a variety of protein rich foods

Protein is essential for the growth and development of your baby. Eat two to three portions of protein rich foods every day including lean meat, poultry, seafood, eggs, legumes, tofu, nuts and seeds.

Consuming one to two portions of oily fish (such as sardines or salmon) per week is advised. It is best to limit oily fish intake to no more than this as some fish may contain pollutants which can accumulate with high intakes and cause a negative health effect. Avoid fish that contain high levels of mercury, including shark, swordfish, marlin and king mackerel, as they can affect your baby's nervous system.

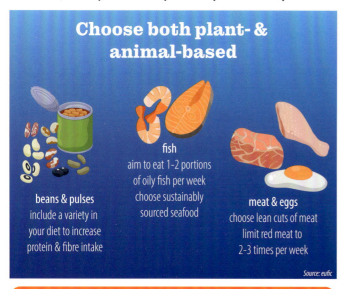

Choose both plant- & animal-based

beans & pulses
include a variety in your diet to increase protein & fibre intake

fish
aim to eat 1-2 portions of oily fish per week choose sustainably sourced seafood

meat & eggs
choose lean cuts of meat limit red meat to 2-3 times per week

Source: eufic

Nutrient highlight: iron

Iron deficiency during pregnancy can impair the growth of your baby. Since many women of childbearing age may be at risk of low iron levels,4 these are often checked during pregnancy and supplements may be advised if body stores are low.

However, by focusing on eating a variety of iron-rich foods, you should be able to get all the iron you need from foods. Foods high in iron include red meat such as beef, lamb and pork. Plant sources include spinach, pulses and whole grain cereals. Iron from plant sources are less readily absorbed by the body than those from animal foods. Iron absorption can be increased from plant sources by eating them with foods rich in vitamin C, like fruits and vegetables. The European Food Safety Authority (EFSA) does not recommend an increased iron intake as a default during pregnancy. However, since many women of childbearing age may be at risk of low iron levels, these are often checked during pregnancy. Your doctor or midwife can advise you if supplements are needed.

Eat dairy foods or fortified alternatives

Dairy foods are rich in protein and many vitamins and minerals, such as calcium, iodine and riboflavin, which play an important role in pregnancy. Try to eat two to three portions of dairy foods every day including milk, unsweetened yoghurts, cheese and dairy alternatives. Those who choose to avoid animal products can opt for alternative plant-based calcium sources such as fortified soya or nut products.

Many cheeses are safe to eat during pregnancy, but you should avoid soft unpasteurised cheeses as these may contain bacteria which can be harmful to your developing baby.

Eat dairy foods or fortified alternatives

yogurt
125 ml

milk
200 ml

cheese
index finger

choose low-fat & unsweetened products

if avoiding dairy, choose fortified alternatives

Source: eufic

Nutrient highlight: calcium

Calcium has many functions during pregnancy and is especially important for the growth of strong bones. Foods rich in calcium include dairy products such as milk, yoghurt, and cheese. Plant sources include tofu, green leafy vegetables and fortified foods. For most people, foods should provide all the calcium the body needs. However, calcium supplements may be advised if body stores are low or dietary intake is below recommended levels. Always consult your general practitioner (GP) before taking any supplements during pregnancy.

Replace saturated fats with unsaturated fats

Fats are an important part of a healthy diet, but not all fats have the same effect on health. You should try to limit intake of foods high in saturated fat such as fatty meats or tropical oils like coconut oil by replacing them with foods rich in unsaturated fats such as unsalted nuts, avocado, oily fish and plant oils like olive or rapeseed oil.

Drink plenty of fluids

Hydration is important for overall health. During pregnancy, drinking plenty of fluids can also help to reduce the chance of constipation and urinary tract infections. On average, pregnant women need around 2 litres of water per day from both food and drinks. During pregnancy, this increases to 2.3 litres per day. As 20-30% of the water we consume comes from foods, you should aim to drink around 1.6 - 1.8 litres of water per day – around 8 glasses.

All drinks will provide hydration, but just like the general population, you should try to limit intakes of sugar-sweetened drinks. Water is the best choice. Other drinks such as milk and caffeine-free tea are also good options. Coffee and other caffeinated drinks are safe to drink as long as you stay under the daily maximum recommended intake of 200 mg of caffeine per day – that's equivalent to 2 cups of coffee a day.

Should I take any supplements when pregnant?

While, a healthy and balanced diet during pregnancy will provide most of the vitamins and minerals you and your baby need, for some nutrients, such as folate and vitamin D, it can be hard to get enough from food alone. Therefore, a supplement is often recommended. Always consult a dietitian or your general practitioner (GP) before taking prenatal supplements.

Folate or Folic acid

Folate or folic acid (the synthetic form of folate) helps to protect against neural tube defects (NTDs), such as spina bifida. NTDs occur when the neural tube fails to form properly during the early stages of pregnancy. This prevents the normal development of the baby's brain and/or spinal cord. Supplementing with folic acid can greatly reduce the risk of NTDs.

Folate is found in many foods such as oranges, green leafy vegetables and whole grains. Unfortunately, folate is not as well absorbed as folic acid and levels found in food are too low to reach recommended levels pre-pregnancy and during the first 12 weeks of development. For this reason, folic acid supplements are advised when trying to conceive and during pregnancy. As pregnancies can be unplanned, sexually-active women of childbearing age are advised to take a daily 400 microgram folic acid supplement.

Vitamin D

Vitamin D has many functions in the body, including helping in the absorption of calcium and supporting the formation of healthy bones. We can get vitamin D from three places; the body can make it from sunlight, we can get it from foods such as fatty fish, eggs, and fortified foods or we can get it from a supplement.

The European Food Safety Authority recommends all adults to get 15 µg of vitamin D a day. During summer months most adults can make enough vitamin D from moderate sun exposure (15 – 30 minutes a day). However, during winter or for people with dark skin or limited sun exposure it can be difficult to reach recommended levels. Although some foods contain vitamin D, levels are often too low to meet our requirements. For this reason, a supplement is often recommended. A vitamin D supplement of 10 to 25 µg a day has been shown to be beneficial during pregnancy, particularly during winter months or for if you have a low level of sun exposure.

A balanced diet for a healthy pregnancy

A healthy balanced diet should provide most of the nutrients you and your developing baby need. There is no 'best' diet for pregnancy and but people should try to eat a variety of foods to meet their nutrient needs. Special care should be taken to eat enough foods that contain calcium, iron and omega-3 fatty acids.

Healthy pregnancy: foods to avoid when pregnant

A nutritious and balanced diet is an important part of a healthy pregnancy. However, certain foods and drinks can increase the risk of harm to your unborn baby. Knowing which foods to avoid and choosing safe alternatives will ensure both your own and your baby's health. However, if you have accidentally eaten something potentially risky, there is still a low chance that it will cause harm. If you are worried about your intake or develop symptoms of food poisoning, always contact your doctor who can further advise you.

Why should pregnant people avoid certain foods?

During pregnancy it is important to avoid some foods that could cause harm to the unborn baby. Some components of food or supplements, as well as infectious agents like bacteria and their toxins, viruses or parasites, may cause foodborne illness, also known as food poisoning.

Food poisoning is usually mild and will only show mild flu-like and gastrointestinal symptoms such as fever, vomiting or diarrhoea. However, as the immune system changes during pregnancy, pregnant people are at greater risk of getting ill from certain infectious agents such as listeria in foods than the general population. Furthermore, some illness-causing microbes can be harmful to a fetus. The overall risks of getting foodborne illnesses are low, and by carefully choosing and preparing your food you can lower your risk even further.

The following foods are best avoided or limited during pregnancy.

Raw/unpasteurised cheeses and milk

Pasteurisation is a process where heat is applied to kill potentially harmful bacteria. During pregnancy, it is

Safe

hard cheeses, pasteurised soft cheeses & pasteurised milk
e.g. parmesan, gruyere, feta, mozzarella & cream cheese

Avoid or cook

soft cheeses & raw milk
e.g. brie, camembert, soft goat's cheese, blue cheese

Source: eufic

therefore advised to stay away from unpasteurised milk and cream, as well as all mould-ripened soft cheeses with a white rind made from unpasteurised (raw) milk, including brie, camembert, chèvre (a type of goats' cheese), roquefort, gorgonzola and Danish blue cheeses. These cheeses may contain Listeria, a bacteria that can cause an illness called listeriosis. Unpasteurised cheeses are safe when they are cooked thoroughly, for example on a pizza or quiche.

Other cheeses are still safe to eat! You can eat all soft cheeses made from pasteurised milk, such as quark, feta, cottage cheese, cream cheese, mozzarella and cheese spreads.

All hard cheeses are safe to eat, even when they are made from unpasteurised milk. These cheeses, such as parmesan and gruyere, contain less water which makes it less likely for bacteria to survive and grow.

Raw or undercooked meat, cured meats and poultry

Undercooked or raw meats, including raw cured meats like salami, chorizo and Parma ham, can contain harmful parasites like Toxoplasma gondii or bacteria like Salmonella or Listeria. You can prevent yourself from becoming ill by always making sure to cook your meat completely, until the centre reaches at least 72°C, with no traces of blood. Avoid cross-contamination of foods by thoroughly washing hands, knives and cutting boards after preparing raw meats in your kitchen and always using different utensils for raw and cooked foods.

Raw or undercooked eggs

Raw eggs can carry the Salmonella bacteria which can cause foodborne illness. Salmonella cannot survive at high temperatures. Cook your eggs thoroughly, to make them safe to eat. Avoid foods that contain raw eggs such as homemade mayonnaises and some desserts. You can still eat mayonnaises, dressings and ice cream sold in supermarkets as they are made with pasteurized eggs and thus safe to eat.

Raw or undercooked seafood and fish high in mercury

You can also still enjoy eating seafood as long as it is well cooked through, to avoid food poisoning. Foods with raw fish and shellfish, such as sushi, sashimi and taramasalata, as well as shelled crustaceans such as shrimps and crabs that

are sold pre-cooked and require cold storage, should be avoided.

Eating fish is encouraged during pregnancy because it is a great source of healthy fatty acids. However, some varieties of fish that are high in mercury should be avoided because too much mercury can cause harm. This includes most predatory fishes such as shark, swordfish, marlin and king mackerel.

Eating two portions of low-mercury fish a week poses no increased risk to the unborn baby. You can limit your intake of mercury by opting for fish with low levels of mercury such as salmon, cod, haddock, plaice, shrimp, anchovies, herring or prawns. Also limit your intake of tuna to one serving of fresh or 4 servings of canned tuna per week.

Raw sprouts, ready-to-eat salads

Eating raw sprouts can be risky during pregnancy. Raw sprouts, for example bean, alfalfa, and radish sprouts, as well as ready-to eat salads can contain harmful bacteria such as Listeria, Salmonella and E. coli. Washing sprouts is not enough to make sure they are safe to eat raw. To kill the harmful bacteria, they must be cooked thoroughly.

You can still eat bagged and pre-washed lettuce and vegetables, as long as you store them in the fridge and give them another wash before consuming them.

In general, vegetables and fruits are safe to eat and are an important part of a healthy diet during pregnancy. However, remember to always wash them thoroughly before eating or preparing them to remove any trace of soil. There is a small chance that unwashed fruits and vegetables could be contaminated with harmful bacteria or parasites like Toxoplasma gondii.

Liver (products) and vitamin A supplements

Avoid eating all liver (products), as liver is high in vitamin A. Some studies have linked large amounts of vitamin A to birth defects and liver damage. It is therefore also not recommended to take any dietary supplement that contains a high dosage of vitamin A during pregnancy.

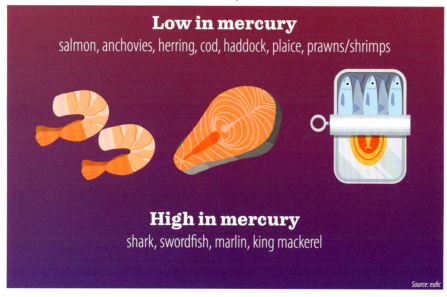

Low in mercury

salmon, anchovies, herring, cod, haddock, plaice, prawns/shrimps

High in mercury

shark, swordfish, marlin, king mackerel

Source: eufic

How much caffeine is found in different products*

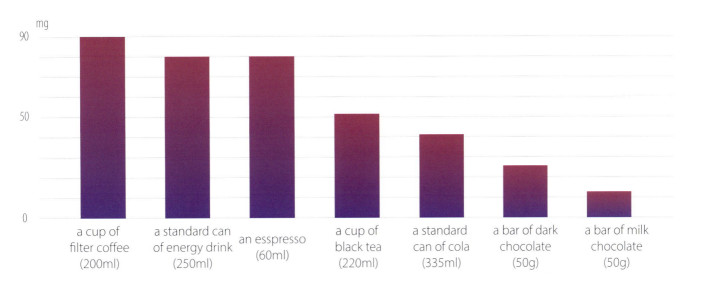

	mg
90	
50	
0	

a cup of filter coffee (200ml) · a standard can of energy drink (250ml) · an esspresso (60ml) · a cup of black tea (220ml) · a standard can of cola (335ml) · a bar of dark chocolate (50g) · a bar of milk chocolate (50g)

* all values are estimations; the caffeine content of food and drinks may

Source: eufic

Pâté should also be avoided, as it can contain the bacteria Listeria and hepatitis E virus.

Alcohol

Drinking alcohol is not safe at any stage during pregnancy and there is no safe level of alcohol consumption during pregnancy. Alcohol can pass through the placenta and the baby will be exposed to the alcohol in the blood. As the baby's liver is not yet fully developed, the alcohol will not be broken down quickly and in turn can affect the baby's development.

However, if you have been drinking occasionally before realising you were pregnant you should stop drinking once you find out you are pregnant. Talk to your doctor if you are concerned about the effects of your alcohol use before you knew you were pregnant.

The more you drink during pregnancy, the greater the risks. Drinking during pregnancy can cause fetal alcohol syndrome (FAS), a serious condition where the baby has severe life-long mental and physical problems.

Caffeine

During pregnancy, it is recommended to limit caffeine intake to 200 mg a day from all sources. A cup of filter coffee (200 ml) contains around 90 mg of caffeine. Caffeine can also naturally be found in tea, chocolate and some soft- and energy drinks. Although the risks are small, high intakes of caffeine (>300 mg per day) during pregnancy have been associated with an increased risk of low birth weight. Further, some evidence suggests that high levels of caffeine may be linked to increased risk of miscarriage and stillbirth so it is best to stick below the maximum recommended safe limit of 200 mg per day.

If you are a heavy coffee drinker, try to gradually lower your consumption or replace coffee with caffeine free teas.

Eating with peace of mind throughout pregnancy

Although there are some foods you have to pay attention to during pregnancy, there are still many foods left to enjoy! Do not worry if you have accidently eaten something potentially risky. The chances that it will cause harm are very small. However, always contact your doctor if you are worried or if you experience symptoms that may indicate food poisoning, such as vomiting, fever or diarrhoea.

1 August 2021

The above information is reprinted with kind permission from EUFIC.
© 2021 EUFIC

www.eufic.org

Mental health in pregnancy

Being pregnant is a big life event and it is natural to feel a lot of different emotions. But if you're feeling sad and it's starting to affect your life, there are things you can try that may help.

Things you can try to help with your mental health

Do

✓ talk about your feelings to a friend, family member, doctor or midwife

✓ try calming breathing exercises if you feel overwhelmed

✓ do physical activity if you can – it can improve your mood and help you sleep

✓ eat a healthy diet with regular meals

✓ try to attend antenatal classes to meet other pregnant people

Don't

✗ do not compare yourself to other pregnant people – everyone experiences pregnancy in different ways

✗ do not be afraid to tell healthcare professionals how you are feeling – they are there to listen and support you

✗ do not use alcohol, cigarettes or drugs to try and feel better – these can make you feel worse and affect your baby's growth and wellbeing

Apps

You may find that some apps can help your mental health. The NHS Apps library has pregnancy and baby apps and mental health apps.

Speak to your midwife or a doctor if:

Things you're trying yourself are not helping

They will offer you more support. They may offer you a referral to perinatal mental health services or other emotional support. Perinatal means the time you are pregnant and up to 12 months after giving birth.

Treatment

The two types of treatment for mental health problems in pregnancy are talking therapies and medicine.

Talking therapies can help with common mental health problems like stress, anxiety and depression.

If you decide to take medicine while you are pregnant your doctor will explain how this may affect your baby. Try not to worry – you will be offered the safest medicine at the lowest amount that will still work.

You may also find it hard to cope with your body changing shape, particularly if you have had an eating disorder.

19 February 2021

The above information is reprinted with kind permission from the NHS.
© Crown copyright 2021
This information is licensed under the Open Government Licence v3.0
To view this licence, visit http://www.nationalarchives.gov.uk/doc/open-government-licence/ **OGL**

www.nhs.uk

Mental health problems

There are many mental health problems you could experience in pregnancy. They can happen at any time, even if this is not your first pregnancy.

If you	You may have
feel sad all the time	Depression
have flashbacks, nightmares or feel intense distress when reminded of a past experience	post-traumatic stress disorder (PTSD) – this can happen if you had a pregnancy go wrong, a traumatic birth or have experienced abuse
have sudden attacks of panic or fear	panic disorder
have obsessive thoughts and compulsive behaviours	obsessive compulsive disorder (OCD)
have an intense fear of giving birth	Tokophobia

Antenatal checks and tests

During your pregnancy, you'll be offered a range of tests, including blood tests and ultrasound baby scans.

These are designed to:

♦ help make your pregnancy safer

♦ check and assess the development and wellbeing of you and your baby

♦ screen for particular conditions

You do not have to have any of the tests – it's your choice. However, it's important to understand the purpose of all tests so you can make an informed decision about whether to have them. You can discuss this with your maternity team.

Weight and height checks in pregnancy

You'll be weighed at your booking appointment, but you will not be weighed regularly during your pregnancy. Your height and weight are used to calculate your body mass index (BMI).

If you are overweight you have an increased risk of problems during pregnancy.

You're likely to put on 10 to 12.5kg (22 to 28lb) in pregnancy after being 20 weeks pregnant. Much of the extra weight is because the baby is growing, but your body also stores fat for making breast milk after birth.

Talk to a GP or midwife if you are concerned about your weight.

It's important to have a healthy diet in pregnancy and do regular exercise during your pregnancy.

Antenatal urine tests

You'll be asked to give a urine sample at your antenatal appointments. Your urine is checked for several things, including protein.

If this is found in your urine, it may mean you have a urine infection. It may also be a sign of pre-eclampsia.

Blood pressure tests in pregnancy

Your blood pressure will be checked at every antenatal visit. A rise in blood pressure later in pregnancy could be a sign of pre-eclampsia.

It's very common for your blood pressure to be lower in the middle of your pregnancy than at other times. This is not a problem, but it may make you feel light-headed if you get up quickly. Talk to your midwife if you're concerned about it.

Blood tests and scans in pregnancy

As part of your antenatal care, you'll be offered several blood tests and scans. Some are offered to everyone, while others are only offered if you might be at risk of a particular infection or condition.

All the tests are done to make your pregnancy safer or check that the baby is healthy, but you do not have to have them if you do not want to.

Blood group and rhesus status

You will be offered a blood test to tell you whether you are blood group rhesus negative or rhesus positive. If you are rhesus negative you may need extra care to reduce the risk of rhesus disease.

Rhesus disease can happen if you are rhesus negative and pregnant and involves your body developing antibodies that attack the baby's blood cells. This can lead to anaemia and jaundice in the baby.

If you are rhesus negative, you may be offered injections during pregnancy to prevent you from producing these antibodies. This is safe for both mother and baby.

Iron deficiency anaemia

Iron deficiency anaemia makes you tired and less able to cope with loss of blood when you give birth.

You should be offered screening for iron deficiency anaemia at your booking appointment and at 28 weeks.

If tests show you have iron deficiency anaemia, you'll probably be offered iron and folic acid.

Gestational diabetes

You may be at higher risk of developing diabetes in pregnancy (gestational diabetes) if you:

♦ are overweight

♦ have had diabetes in pregnancy before

♦ have had a baby weighing 4.5kg (9.9lb) or more before

♦ have a close relative with diabetes

♦ have a south Asian, black or African Caribbean, or Middle Eastern family background

If you're considered to be at high risk for gestational diabetes, you may be offered a test called the OGTT (oral glucose tolerance test). This involves drinking a sugary drink and having blood tests.

The OGTT is done when you're between 24 and 28 weeks pregnant. If you've had gestational diabetes before, you'll be offered:

♦ early self monitoring of blood glucose levels, or

♦ an OGTT earlier in pregnancy, soon after your booking visit, and another at 24 to 28 weeks if the first test is normal

30 November 2020

The above information is reprinted with kind permission from the NHS.
© Crown copyright 2021
This information is licensed under the Open Government Licence v3.0
To view this licence, visit http://www.nationalarchives.gov.uk/doc/open-government-licence/ **OGL**

www.nhs.uk

If antenatal screening tests find something

Most antenatal screening tests will not find anything, but there's a chance you'll be told your baby could be born with a condition. If this happens to you, there's always support available.

Get as much information as you can

It can help to find out as much as you can about the condition your baby may have.

A specialist doctor (obstetrician) or midwife will explain what the screening results mean and talk to you about your options.

Your appointments

Your appointments should take place in a private and quiet space. But this can sometimes be difficult in a busy hospital.

You can bring your partner, a family member or friend with you.

It might help to write down any questions you have before you go. Ask the doctor or midwife to explain anything again if you need them to.

You could ask things like:

♦ Can you explain what my baby may have?

♦ What would that mean for my baby?

♦ Will we need any special care or treatment before birth?

♦ What would life be like for my baby if they have this condition?

Next steps

You may be offered further tests (sometimes called diagnostic tests).

These tests check if your baby definitely has the condition screening tests have said they might have.

The tests you may be offered are:

♦ amniocentesis

♦ chorionic villus sampling (CVS)

You may also have further scans.

It's up to you to decide if you want to do any further tests. You can discuss this with a doctor or midwife.

Important: In most cases, you'll find out if your baby has the condition they were tested for. But in some cases this may not be possible.

Making a decision to continue with or end your pregnancy

This can be a very difficult decision. You may find you feel differently from one day to the next.

You do not have to make this decision on your own. Speak to your doctor, midwife, family and friends about your options.

You have time to think about your decision – whatever you decide, you'll have support.

Support is available

It can help to speak to:

♦ your partner, family or friends

♦ a midwife or specialist doctor

♦ a local support group

♦ charities that support families with your baby's condition

♦ a counsellor – you do not need a referral from your GP (find out more about how to see a counsellor)

3 April 2019

The above information is reprinted with kind permission from the NHS.
© Crown copyright 2021
This information is licensed under the Open Government Licence v3.0
To view this licence, visit http://www.nationalarchives.gov.uk/doc/open-government-licence/ **OGL**

www.nhs.uk

The decision is yours to make.

But you don't have to be alone to make it.

Pregnancy loss statistics

The latest UK statistics about pregnancy loss and complications.

Every baby deserves the best start in life, and we are committed to funding medical research and providing information to help more mums and dads have a healthy pregnancy and birth.

- Around 60,000 babies are born prematurely each year in the UK.

- In the UK, it is estimated that 1 in 4 pregnancies end in loss during pregnancy or birth.

Key statistics about pregnancy and loss in the UK

- 712,680 births were registered in 2019 (640,370 England & Wales; 49,863 Scotland; 22,447 Northern Ireland)

- There were 2,763 stillbirths in 2019 (2,522 England & Wales; 174 Scotland; 67 Northern Ireland)

- Approximately 60,000 babies were born prematurely in 2019

- An estimated 1 in 5 pregnancies ended in miscarriage (1 in 8 if we only count women who realised/reported the miscarriage)

- Estimates suggest there are 250,000 miscarriages every year in the UK, and around 11,000 emergency admissions for ectopic pregnancies

- There were 2,131 neonatal deaths in 2019

- 114 women died from mental health-related causes during or up to one year after pregnancy in the UK and Ireland in 2018

- 209 women died during or up to 6 weeks after pregnancy between 2015-2017 - this equates to 9.2 women per 100,000 who died due to causes associated with pregnancy during pregnancy or soon after.

The above information is reprinted with kind permission from Tommy's.
© 2021 Tommy's

www.tommys.org

Each day in 2018

2,060 babies

were born alive

515 babies were miscarried

144 babies were born preterm

8 babies were stillborn

Source: Tommy's

Signs of a miscarriage: should I be worried?

Once you've confirmed the result on a pregnancy test, being pregnant is a nerve-wracking time for all mums-to-be and miscarriage is a worry that crops up for many of us, causing confusion and fear. But what exactly are the signs of a miscarriage?

A miscarriage is the name given when a pregnancy ends before 24 weeks. If you miscarry in the first 12 weeks of pregnancy (the first trimester), it is called an 'early miscarriage' – around three quarters happen in this initial stage when some women don't yet realise they're pregnant. A miscarriage after the 12-week mark is called a 'late miscarriage'.

Signs of a miscarriage

1. Vaginal bleeding

The most common symptom of miscarriage is vaginal bleeding. You'd either have a light brown discharge, or heavy bleeding and bright red blood that gradually reduces to a stop after a few days. Light vaginal bleeding during your first trimester of pregnancy is common, so try not to automatically jump into panic mode. Still contact your maternity team or early pregnancy unit at your local hospital immediately, just to be sure everything's ok.

If, however, you experience heavy and painful bleeding, severe abdominal pain and are feeling faint and light-headed you should immediately go to your nearest A&E department.

2. Cramping and pain

While some light cramps and pain in your stomach area during early pregnancy isn't unusual (after all, your womb is expanding for your baby!), cramping and pain in your lower abdomen may be caused by a miscarriage so it's worth contacting your midwife to get checked out.

3. Discharge of fluid or tissue from your vagina

As with vaginal bleeding, some women pass white-pink discharge while pregnant which may be a cause for concern.

4. Intuition

Don't underestimate how well you know your own body. Unfortunately, some women find they have no physical signs of miscarriage and instead simply have 'a feeling'. It is entirely reasonable to contact your midwife if you are concerned.

While symptoms of pregnancy tend to decrease naturally as you move into your second trimester, if you were previously experiencing pregnancy symptoms such as a feeling sick or having tender breasts and these are no longer present early on in your pregnancy, contact your midwife for advice.

What causes a miscarriage?

The NHS estimates that up to two thirds of early miscarriages are related to chromosome abnormalities. A fetus needs to have 23 chromosomes (blocks of DNA-carrying genes) from the father's sperm and 23 from the mother's egg to make a full set.

Abnormalities often happen when a baby receives the wrong number of chromosomes. Problems with the development of the placenta or the fetus developing outside the womb can also lead to a miscarriage.

Diana Hamilton-Fairley, consultant in obstetrics and gynaecology and advisor to the Miscarriage Association, says, 'It's nothing inherited, just bad luck and no-one's fault. Part of the process has gone wrong though we're unlikely to know what.'

A late miscarriage – after 12 weeks – could be down to health problems such as diabetes, infection, severe high blood pressure and problems with the cervix, uterus or placenta. But, pinning down exactly why you've miscarried can be tricky.

When can a miscarriage happen?

The majority of miscarriages happen during the earlier weeks of pregnancy before the 12 week mark. You may experience different signs and symptoms of a miscarriage depending on how far along you are in your pregnancy journey.

Miscarriage at week 5, week 6, week 7 and week 8

We spoke to Dr Eleni Mavrides, Consultant Obstetrician and Gynaecologist at The Portland Hospital, part of HCA Healthcare UK, to find out more about how miscarriage symptoms can vary from week to week.

'Broadly, there are two key time frames for a miscarriage to occur: an early miscarriage in the first 12 weeks, or a late miscarriage in the final 12 to 24 weeks. Whilst miscarriage symptoms do not significantly vary week by week, they do sightly differ between the early and late miscarriage stages.'

About 3 in every 4 miscarriages happen during the 'early miscarriage' stage. For an early miscarriage which occurs between conception and week 12 of pregnancy, the most common symptoms you would expect to see include:

♦ Vaginal bleeding (however, do note that a little light bleeding is common during the early stages of pregnancy, and does not always mean you are experiencing a miscarriage).

♦ Cramps in the lower abdomen which feel like bad period pains.

♦ Unfamiliar fluid or tissue coming out of the vagina.

♦ Pregnancy symptoms previously being experienced have disappeared, for example, morning sickness has stopped and the breasts no longer feel sore or tender.

Miscarriage after 12 weeks

Whilst it is more uncommon to miscarry in the later stage of pregnancy, the symptoms that one might experience if they miscarry in weeks 12 to 24 of pregnancy include all the above, as well as:

♦ Heavy bleeding and blood clots from the vagina.

♦ Extremely painful cramps in the lower abdomen or back.

♦ An inability to feel any movement from the foetus if they had previously been feeling movement.

If you are experiencing any of these symptoms it is important that you seek medical attention immediately.

What affects your chances of having a miscarriage?

Research suggests that age does play a role. Women under 30 have a one in 10 chance of having a pregnancy end in miscarriage, while women between 35 and 39 have a one in five chance, according to the NHS. If you are an older mum-to-be, however, you still have a very good chance of delivering a healthy baby to term.

Other factors affecting your chance of miscarriage include smoking, alcohol and excessive caffeine. Doctors recommend no more than 200mg of caffeine in a day (that's around two mugs of instant coffee) and to limit yourself to two units of alcohol a week (equivalent to a small glass of wine).

The main thing to remember in any case is that feeling grief, shock and pain is completely normal, so don't be afraid to take the time you need and accept the support around you.

The search for the causes of miscarriage

Most parents never find out why their miscarriage happened. Tommy's, the largest charity funding research into miscarriage, stillbirth and premature birth, is working to improve understanding of the biological processes at work, and finding ways to prevent miscarriages not caused by chromosomal abnormalities.

What does a miscarriage look and feel like?

In many cases you won't know you've had a miscarriage – it happens before you even know you're pregnant.

If you've had your pregnancy confirmed then bleeding – ranging from brownish discharge to heavy bleeding – and period-like pain are common signs. Sometimes women no longer feel sick and their breasts are no longer tender.

'If you've had any of those symptoms you mustn't assume it's miscarriage,' Diana says. 'It could be a little blood from the placenta or, if you've recently had sex it could be blood from the cells on the surface of the cervix that are more delicate in pregnancy.

'And nausea and breast tenderness tend to disappear around 12 weeks anyway.'

You might be wondering what is actually happening to your body during a miscarriage. Dr Eleni has described what happens in the womb to help us understand our bodies and the symptoms.

'During a miscarriage, the cervix, which is essentially the "neck" of the womb, softens to allow material from inside the womb pass through. This is often seen in the form of bleeding, fluids, and tissues coming out of the vagina. However, sometimes the womb is unable to clean itself, or may still have the foetus inside if the miscarriage

has occurred in the later stages, requiring the intervention of medical professionals.'

How long does a miscarriage last?

A woman early in her pregnancy may have a miscarriage and only experience bleeding and cramping for a few hours. But another woman may have miscarriage bleeding for up to a week. The bleeding can be heavy with clots, but it slowly tapers off over days before stopping, usually within two weeks.

The length of a miscarriage differs for every woman, and depends on different factors, including: how far along you were in the pregnancy, whether you were carrying multiples and how long it takes your body to expel the fetal tissue and placenta.

What should I do if I'm worried I am miscarrying?

Contact your GP. He/she will examine you to see if the neck of your womb is opening. If they're concerned they'll send you to hospital where you may be given an ultrasound (sometimes performed using a small probe inside the vagina which will not increase your risk of miscarriage if your pregnancy is actually safe) to check the baby's heartbeat and development. You may also be given a blood test to measure the hormone levels associated with pregnancy.

If you are miscarrying then sadly there's nothing that can be done to stop it but it's reassuring to know that should you decide to try again you have exactly the same chance of having a normal pregnancy as before.

Is there anything I can do to prevent miscarriage?

'We know that being overweight makes it harder to push sugar out of your bloodstream and this seems to affect the development of the baby so if you're considering pregnancy it might be worth losing a few pounds,' Diana says. 'We also know that smoking and drinking isn't a good idea.'

Eat a healthy diet with plenty of fruit and vegetables and carry on exercising in moderation, she says. While it's unwise to go from nothing to a marathon overnight there's evidence to suggest gentle exercise – walking and swimming for example – is healthy during pregnancy.

What is a missed miscarriage?

A missed (or silent) miscarriage is one where the baby has died or not developed but has not been physically miscarried yet. In many cases, there has been no sign that anything was wrong - you will most likely find out at your scan, so the news can come as a complete shock. With a silent miscarriage, you likely won't have any side effects. Brownish discharge might be present on some occasions. Some women also experience a loss of their pregnancy symptoms.

How common is a missed miscarriage?

Approximately 1-5% of all pregnancies will result in a missed miscarriage.

If you have a missed miscarriage your doctor will explain the next options. You can either:

1. Wait for the miscarriage to happen by itself naturally
2. You can also take medication to help things along
3. Or, you may need to have surgery to remove the pregnancy.

Your GP will talk with you about what may be the best option for you. Take some time before you decide to let the diagnosis sink in.

Who can I talk to?

Whoever you reach out to, the most important thing is to reach out to someone. Whether that be your partner, a friend, family. While it is a devastating thing to experience, sharing these experiences is vital to understand that you're not alone. There are numerous phonelines, websites and people who will listen and understand what you're going through. Above all, do not lose hope.

'Remember there's an 85% chance you won't suffer a miscarriage and bear in mind even a woman who has had three miscarriages still stands a 65% chance of her next pregnancy being successful,' Diana says.

The above information is reprinted with kind permission from *Mother & Baby*.
© 2021 Bauer Media Group

www.motherandbaby.co.uk

What is an Ectopic Pregnancy?

Ectopic pregnancy is a common, occasionally life-threatening condition that affects 1 in 80 pregnancies. Put very simply, it means "an out-of-place pregnancy".

What is an ectopic pregnancy?

It occurs when an ovum (egg) that has been fertilised implants (gets stuck) outside the cavity of the uterus (womb). The most common place for an ectopic pregnancy is the Fallopian tube but there are many other sites where an ectopic pregnancy can be located. It is, sadly, not possible to move an ectopic pregnancy into the uterus.

Each month, during the menstrual cycle, ovulation occurs where one of the ovaries produces an egg that is drawn into the end of the Fallopian tube by finger-like structures called fimbriae. The egg then makes its way along the Fallopian tube towards the uterus. During the course of this journey, if intercourse (sex) has occurred, it may encounter sperm, in which case it may become fertilised.

If it is fertilised, the egg implants itself into the lining of the uterus called the 'endometrium' and ultimately grows into a baby. If it is not fertilised, then both the egg and uterus lining are discharged in the menstrual flow (period), a fresh lining is prepared, and a new egg begins to mature within the ovary.

With an ectopic pregnancy, the fertilised egg becomes caught or delayed while progressing along the Fallopian tube. In this case, the pregnancy continues to grow inside the Fallopian tube where it can cause the Fallopian tube to burst or severely damage it. This can sometimes cause internal bleeding causing pain and requiring immediate medical attention.

How many are affected by the condition?

Each year in the UK nearly 12,000 women have ectopic pregnancies diagnosed (Source: *The 2016 MBRRACE Confidential Enquiries into Maternal Deaths and Morbidity 2009–14*). From anecdotal evidence, it is believed the number of cases of ectopic pregnancy may number more than 30,000 per year in the UK alone.

According to the *2019 MBRRACE Maternal Deaths and Morbidity Report 2015-17*, of the women who died from early pregnancy problems, all but one had ectopic pregnancies and all died within 48 hours of presentation with their ectopic pregnancy.

Sadly, there are on average two deaths per year in the UK and Ireland due to ectopic pregnancy. In the 21st century, no woman should die of an ectopic pregnancy. Depending on individual medical circumstances, several treatments are available. The pregnancy can never be saved.

The Ectopic Pregnancy Trust believes that the deaths and trauma associated with ectopic pregnancy should be prevented. We seek to relieve the distress associated with the experience and provide ongoing support through their treatment and beyond.

What are the different types of ectopic pregnancy?

95% are in the Fallopian tube – either ampullary (in the middle part of the Fallopian tube), isthmic (in the upper part

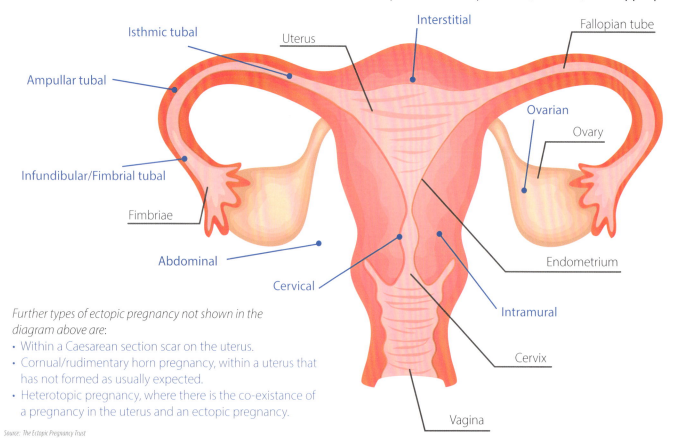

Further types of ectopic pregnancy not shown in the diagram above are:

- Within a Caesarean section scar on the uterus.
- Cornual/rudimentary horn pregnancy, within a uterus that has not formed as usually expected.
- Heterotopic pregnancy, where there is the co-existance of a pregnancy in the uterus and an ectopic pregnancy.

Source: The Ectopic Pregnancy Trust

of the Fallopian tube close to the uterus) or fimbrial (at the end of the tube)

♦   3% are interstitial (inside the part of the Fallopian tube that crosses into the uterus)

♦   < 1% are within a Caesarean section scar on the uterus

♦   < 1% are cervical (on the cervix)

♦   < 1% are cornual (within an abnormally shaped uterus)

♦   < 1% are ovarian (in or on the ovary)

♦   < 1% are intramural (in the muscle of the uterus)

♦   < 1% are abdominal (in the abdomen)

♦   < 1% are heterotopic pregnancies

The image shows where ectopic pregnancies are most likely to occur.

Symptoms of an ectopic pregnancy

Ectopic pregnancy is a common, occasionally life-threatening condition that affects 1 in 80 pregnancies. This page provides detailed general information on symptoms and, if a person is experiencing any or all of these signs, they should seek medical attention. Please remember that online medical information is no substitute for expert medical care from your own healthcare team.

Symptoms

Lower tummy pain and/or bleeding during pregnancy may be due to a number of causes. It is however very important that an ectopic pregnancy as the cause is excluded. If not diagnosed and treated quickly an ectopic pregnancy can lead to internal bleeding and a medical emergency.

Some experience symptoms that are similar to other conditions such as gastroenteritis (tummy bug) and miscarriage, which are the most common ways to misdiagnose an ectopic pregnancy. Not all experience symptoms.

The diagnosis of ectopic pregnancy may sometimes be difficult, and symptoms may occur from as early as 4 weeks pregnant and up to 12 weeks or even later. In addition, although there are a number of recognised risk factors, in over 50% of women diagnosed with an ectopic pregnancy, there are no identifiable risk factors.

If your instincts are screaming at you that something does not feel right, it is OK to trust them and ask for reassessment at any time. Please do be vigilant and take any pain that concerns you seriously until absolutely proven otherwise.

If you are experiencing any of the following ectopic pregnancy symptoms, please contact your doctor/GP or your local Early Pregnancy Unit. You can also call the NHS Direct 111 service by dialing 111 or access the NHS GP at Hand service. You can contact your out-of-hours doctor/GP service if your normal surgery is closed or go to your local Accident and Emergency department (A&E) or Urgent Care Centre.

A missed or late period

If you have missed one or more periods, the most likely reason is that you have become pregnant, and it is progressing as it should. However, if you experience typical pregnancy symptoms, such as nausea, painful breasts or a swollen abdomen but no bleeding or pain, this does not completely rule out an ectopic pregnancy, although this is rare. A true period should be normal flow and duration for you. A light period may be abnormal bleeding in pregnancy and should be investigated with a pregnancy test.

Vaginal bleeding

Ongoing bleeding that is sometimes red or brown/black and watery (like "prune juice") should be investigated. The bleeding may be heavier or lighter than usual. Prolonged off/on light and sometimes heavy bleeding are quite often seen in ectopic pregnancy and should always prompt a pregnancy test and if positive should be urgently investigated with an Early Pregnancy Unit (EPU) referral.

When seeking medical attention, you will be asked for your last menstrual period which should be your last episode of a normal flow and duration bleeding. It is important that abnormal bleeding does not get confused with a normal period as health care professionals may think you are much less pregnant than you are.

Pregnancy test

Pregnancy test kits that are available now are very sensitive. They can be positive before you have missed your period. It is sensible to perform the test in the morning when urine contains the most pregnancy hormone (Human Chorionic Gonadotrophin or hCG). Very rarely a pregnancy test can give a falsely negative result. This is usually because the hormone level is low. If you do a test and are surprised by a negative result, repeat the test perhaps with a different pregnancy test kit. If it is still negative and you still think you are pregnant, your doctor can do a blood test to measure the hCG accurately.

If you are in pain and/or bleeding and your home pregnancy test is negative, but you think it should be positive, ensure you are seen by a doctor urgently by attending your local Accident & Emergency department or by contacting your specialist Early Pregnancy Unit.

The blood test that doctors would perform is for hCG which is a hormone produced in pregnancy. HCG is commonly detected in urine by using a urinary pregnancy test, which can show as positive or negative. Blood tests can identify the exact hCG level in the blood. Your GP can do this test, but it will take a few days to get the result, while the hospital and EPU will have the result in a few hours. This is why, if you have symptoms and a surprisingly negative urine pregnancy test, it is better to be seen at the hospital.

Abdominal pain

During pregnancy, it is not uncommon to experience a period-like ache in your lower tummy and back. However, the following should be investigated:

♦   One-sided pain in your tummy which may be persistent (which means it continues) or intermittent (which means it comes and goes). The pain may have begun suddenly or been gradual.

♦   Discomfort with bloating and a feeling of fullness (not associated with eating) when lying down, particularly if you have already had a child.

♦   Significant lower abdominal and/or back pain.

Ectopic pregnancy symptom checker

1 in 80

1 in 80 pregnancies

Life threatening condition

Symptoms are similar to miscarriage or upset stomach

Unusual vaginal bleeding

Abdominal pain

Shoulder tip pain

Bowel/bladder problems

Missed/late period

Positive pregnancy test

Feeling faint or collapse

Seek medical attention

Ectopic pregnancy symptoms are similar to those of other conditions.
Any **woman or person capable of concieving** of childbearing age who is **sexually active or undergoing assisted reproductive technology** (ART) treatment, who has **any of these symptoms**, should **seek medical attention** as soon as possible.

Source: The Ectopic Pregnancy Trust

Shoulder tip pain

Shoulder tip pain is exactly where it says – not the neck or the back but the tip of your shoulder. If you look to the left over your shoulder and then cast your eyes down, the tip of your shoulder is where your shoulder ends and your arm starts. Shoulder tip pain is very distinctive. You know when you have it because it is a very weird pain you have probably never experienced before. The pain may have begun suddenly.

Shoulders cause pain when we are stressed because we hold ourselves more rigidly and muscles in the back and neck go in to spasm or you may have slept in an awkward position – this is most likely not shoulder tip pain related to an ectopic pregnancy.

Significant shoulder tip pain tends to develop with other symptoms such as feeling unwell, abdominal pain or vaginal bleeding, faintness, abdominal bloating and fullness, or pain when opening your bowels.

It is caused by internal bleeding irritating the diaphragm (the muscle in your chest which helps you to breathe) when you breathe in and out.

Bladder or bowel problems

Diarrhoea

Pain when you have your bowels open (go for a poo)

Pain when you pass water (have a wee)

Shooting/sharp vaginal pain

Some pain and a change in your normal bladder and bowel pattern are features of a typical pregnancy for some. All the same, if you present at your doctor/GP or Early Pregnancy

Unit with such symptoms, it would be reasonable to have an early pregnancy assessment.

Collapse

Feeling light-headed, or faint, or actually fainting

Often accompanied by sickness and looking pale

Increasing or slowing pulse rate or falling blood pressure may also be present

Get help immediately

If you are experiencing these symptoms with or without shoulder tip pain present, seek urgent medical attention. This may be by calling an ambulance.

Deciding whether your symptoms are getting worse

It is difficult at times to know what symptoms are concerning. If you are at all worried, you should seek medical advice. Contact your doctor/GP or local Early Pregnancy Unit for advice. Your GP will likely refer you to your local Early Pregnancy Unit for an assessment. This may involve a blood test in the first instance or an ultrasound scan dependent on how many weeks pregnant you are and your symptoms.

It is important to remember that pregnancy symptoms are common and that not all experiencing such symptoms have an ectopic pregnancy. However, it is important to be vigilant and if in doubt, seek medical attention and advice.

The above information is reprinted with kind permission from The Ectopic Pregnancy Trust.
© 2021 The Ectopic Pregnancy Trust

www.ectopic.org.uk

'I had no idea stillbirth still happened':
5 things you may not know about baby loss

'I didn't have a clue miscarriage could drag on for so long.'

Individuals who have not experienced pregnancy or baby loss may have a basic understanding of what a miscarriage or stillbirth entails. However, there may still be a lot they don't know, perhaps due to the misconceptions that continue to surround miscarriage and stillbirth.

On Thursday 1 October, Chrissy Teigen shared in a social media post that she had suffered pregnancy loss after experiencing excessive bleeding during pregnancy, saying that she and her husband John Legend are 'shocked and in the kind of deep pain you only hear about, the kind of pain we've never felt before'.

Then, a month later, the Duchess of Sussex, Meghan Markle, spoke candidly about her experience of baby loss in a personal essay for the *New York Times* saying: 'I knew, as I clutched my firstborn child, that I was losing my second.'

The Independent spoke to bereaved parents and experts to share facts people may not know about pregnancy and baby loss.

Miscarriage can occur after 12 weeks

For some parents who are expecting a baby, the 12-week scan marks a turning point during the pregnancy, the point at which they can reveal to their friends and family that a child is on the way.

This may be due to the fact that some believe miscarriages can only occur up to 12 weeks into a pregnancy.

However, this isn't the case, explains Karen Burgess, CEO of baby loss counselling charity Petals.

'Miscarriage can happen any time between 12 and 24 weeks. That's the technical line where after that, it becomes a stillbirth,' Karen states.

Ruth Bender-Atik, national director of the Miscarriage Association, explains that while many adults are aware of how common miscarriage is – occurring on average in one in four pregnancies – 'most people assume everything is ok'.

'We never expect it to happen to us. That's part of the reason why actually miscarrying comes as such a terrible shock, because you really don't think it's going to happen to you,' Ruth states.

The shock of miscarriage also leads some parents to assuming they may be at fault in some way, Tommy's midwife Kate Pinney explains.

'We know the chances of it being something the parents did is almost negligible, but the first thing parents do is blame themselves,' Kate says.

A mother may not realise she has suffered a miscarriage

Those who are aware of what a miscarriage entails may expect a woman who is suffering one to experience early symptoms such as spotting.

However, it is possible for a pregnant woman to have experienced a miscarriage without realising, having not exhibited any symptoms. This is called a 'missed miscarriage'.

'I found out the baby had stopped developing at seven weeks'

'A "missed" or "silent miscarriage" occurs when the baby has died but the pregnancy hormones are still ongoing,' Ruth outlines.

Nicola Rash, a 33-year-old lab manager from Suffolk, experienced two miscarriages. The first happened in 2018 and the second, a year later.

'Everything had seemed perfectly normal. I'd got to 12 weeks pregnant and I'd had all the symptoms of being pregnant. Then one day I was going to a meeting at work and I just felt like something wasn't right,' Nicola says. 'I went to the loo and wiped and there was blood, so obviously I was quite alarmed, and then I started to have cramps.'

The next day, Nicola called her early pregnancy unit and went in for a scan. 'I found out the baby had stopped developing at seven weeks. So I'd been carrying it around in there for five weeks without knowing,' she says.

When a woman experiences a missed miscarriage, they are offered the option to take medicine to help speed up the process. This is called 'medical management'.

According to baby charity Tommy's, medical management is a successful method in 85 per cent of cases of missed miscarriage. However, for some, like Nicola, surgery may also be required.

'I had to be rushed into surgery because I had retained tissue, which is something I didn't know could happen,' Nicola says. 'It's where your body hasn't expelled everything the first time round. It was all quite traumatic.'

Stillbirth is more common than many may think

Alyx Elliott, director of strategy at Petals, experienced the stillbirth of her daughter, Skye, at 37 weeks in 2017. Prior to her experience, Alyx was of the belief that stillbirth was something that no longer occurred in this day and age.

'Before I was pregnant with Skye, I thought stillbirth was something from the Victorian age and before that. I had no idea that it still happened,' Alyx says. 'It staggers me when you actually do look into it just how common it is.'

In 2017, one in every 238 births in the UK was a stillbirth, charity Sands outlines. This equates to nine stillborn babies a day and around 3,200 stillbirths that year.

Dr Clea Harmer, chief executive of the stillbirth and neonatal death charity, explains that many people are under the assumption that the deaths of babies is 'just one of those things'.

'We know that many other countries have lower rates of perinatal mortality than the UK and that there are things we can do to reduce the number of babies dying,' Dr Harmer states.

'I completely thought I was safe'

'Once this misconception is addressed, we will be able to work together to better understand the reasons babies die and to put the necessary changes in place to reduce the perinatal mortality rate.'

Alice Bailey, a paediatric nurse, and Dave Bailey, an IT professional, experienced the stillbirth of their daughter Vera at 38 weeks in 2016. Dave says he believes the main cause of the 'stigma' that surrounds stillbirth is that the fact people 'still think it's rare'.

Alice adds she was previously 'guilty' of thinking pregnant mothers in their last trimester were automatically 'safe'.

'If I saw someone who was in the last trimester I'd be like, "You're safe now, not far to go",' Alice says. 'I remember when I was 37 and a bit weeks with Vera thinking, "I'm so uncomfortable, I just need to get this baby out." I completely thought I was safe.'

Every pregnancy and baby loss experience is different

One of the things that struck Nicola most about miscarriage through her own experiences was how different they can be.

'I always thought that it was just you get the impression that something's not right, and then you start cramping and you bleed, and then you pass the pregnancy,' Nicola says.

'What I didn't realise was that it can drag on for so long, or that you can have miscarried so long before and not have a single clue. There's so many options and medical things you have to think of and deal with, like going for blood tests and choosing how to get rid of your pregnancy, and I just had no idea.'

Ruth, of the Miscarriage Association, explains that it is important to consider the fact that not everyone reacts to miscarriage in the same way.

'For many people, miscarriage is deeply distressing, it may be the worst thing that's happened to them so far in their life. But there are some people who simply say, "You know what, I know miscarriage happens, it's one of those things. I'm sure it'll be ok next time",' she states.

Ruth also outlines how the portrayal of pregnancy and baby loss in film and TV can leave viewers with a misleading idea of what it can entail.

'You get some really powerful portrayals, but I think the thing that people find the most difficult is when you have a highly dramatic miscarriage scene, which tends to show someone falling down the stairs or falling down in the street clutching their stomach in a pool of blood, which generally isn't how miscarriage happens,' Ruth says.

In Alice's opinion, stereotypical depictions of baby loss in soap operas are frequently void of the emotional aftermath.

'I've seen it in a couple of soaps, and I just think it happens and then the couples always seem to recover very quickly,' she says.

'They never talk about the recovery side of things, there's never any counselling or anything. I don't think they've truly nailed how much it breaks you.'

Maternity wards have rooms dedicated to pregnancy and baby loss

When one pictures a maternity ward, they would presumably visualise a hospital ward filled with pregnant women, their families and the sounds of crying, newborn babies.

However, unless an individual has experienced pregnancy or baby loss, they may not realise that it is also the place where some parents first learn of and suffer the deaths of their babies.

I could hear other babies being born and other babies crying

Petals CEO Karen first started working as a baby loss counsellor in 2009. The early stages of her work involved working on the same maternity unit where she had given birth to her children several years prior.

'I suddenly walked through these places seeing through different eyes,' Karen says. 'I didn't realise that part of the maternity ward where people were having their babies were one or two rooms where parents go whose babies are going to die, or have died.

'There's a separate area of the maternity ward for this, but I didn't know that.'

Following the death of her daughter Vera, Alice was looked after in the hospital for a few more days, an experience that she found very upsetting.

'I stayed in the hospital for I think another three days while I recovered, which was horrific because I was on the labour ward,' Alice says.

'I could hear other babies being born and other babies crying. Horrific.'

If you have been affected by any of the issues raised in this article, you can contact stillbirth and neonatal death charity Sands on 0808 164 3332 or email helpline@sands.org.uk. The helpline is open from 9.30am to 5.30pm Monday to Friday, and until 9.30pm on Tuesday and Thursday evenings.

You can contact the Miscarriage Association helpline on 01924 200799 or email the charity at info@miscarriageassociation. org.uk. The helpline is open from 9am to 4pm Monday to Friday.

You can also find bereavement support at The Lullaby Trust by calling 0808 802 6868 or emailing support@lullabytrust. org.uk.

To contact Petals to enquire about the charity's counselling services, you can call 0300 688 0068 or email counselling@ petalscharity.org

25 November 2020

The above information is reprinted with kind permission from *The Independent*.
© independent.co.uk 2021

www.independent.co.uk

Why babies die?

There's a wide range of reasons why babies die. We look at causes of stillbirths (death before birth) and deaths of newborn babies separately as different problems are more common in each group.

Sadly, the death of a baby is not rare. Every day in the UK around 14 babies die before, during or soon after birth. That means nearly every two hours a family is faced with the devastation of the death of their baby.

Stillbirth rates in England and Wales have continued to fall, which is good news. But despite recent improvements, the current trajectory in reducing the rate of stillbirths means the English Government will be a long way off achieving their National Maternity Safety Ambition to reduce stillbirths and neonatal deaths by 50% by 2025.

Figures from MBRRACE-UK show that stillbirth rates are highest for Black women and higher for South Asian and Asian women and for those who live in deprived areas. These inequalities have been further highlighted by Covid-19, and the Government must set a target to reduce these clear inequalities in perinatal mortality.

Stillbirths

Many people think that stillbirths happen because of a developmental or genetic problem that means the baby could not survive. In fact, this is the case for fewer than one in ten stillborn babies. For as many as 35% of stillbirths, the cause of death remains unknown.

Placental problems

The placenta is the organ that joins the baby and mother in the womb, allowing nutrients and oxygen to pass to the baby. Some stillbirths happen because the placenta doesn't function properly. This may happen gradually, and it may not be picked up by current routine antenatal monitoring.

A baby who doesn't get the right balance of nutrients may grow more slowly than expected. So a tailing off of a baby's growth during pregnancy can signal a problem. Babies who are becoming poorly may move less often, too.

Sands helped fund research (the AFFIRM study) that asked whether encouraging women to be aware of their baby's movements and to tell their midwife promptly if their baby's movements have changed could help reduce the number of stillbirths. If you are pregnant and have any concerns about your baby's movements, please contact your maternity unit straight away.

We have also funded research looking at scanning in third trimester, which is aimed at improving methods for identifying babies who are not growing as they should.

Other causes

Other causes of stillbirth include:

- other causes linked to the placenta, such as bleeding
- complications of pre-eclampsia, which causes high blood pressure
- problems with the umbilical cord
- a liver disorder called intrahepatic cholestasis of pregnancy (ICP)

- genetic conditions
- infection.

Incidents during birth

Around 100 babies die every year because of a trauma or event during birth that was not anticipated or well managed. Some babies are stillborn and some die after birth. Many of these deaths, when they occur at term, could be avoided with better care. Recently, with improving NHS care, the number of these deaths is falling.

Neonatal deaths

Neonatal deaths can be linked with:

- prematurity or low birthweight, both of which increase the likelihood of serious health problems
- genetic disorders

How many babies die?

Sadly, the death of a baby is not a rare event: around 14 babies die before, during or soon after birth every day in the UK.

Stillbirths

In the UK in 2019, 2,763 stillbirths occurred, which is around 1 in every 250 births. Meanwhile there were 2,066 neonatal deaths, around one in every 345 births.

Around one-third of stillbirths happen after 37 weeks of pregnancy.

Stillbirths account for more than half of the deaths of infants under one year in the UK.

Stillbirth rates remained largely unchanged from the late 1990s to 2011. From 2012 the rate started to fall. But more deaths could be prevented.

Neonatal deaths

In the UK in 2019, 2,066 babies died within the first four weeks of life. That's one baby in every 345 births

The mortality rate for neonatal babies (the first 28 days after birth) has dropped over the last decade, largely because of advances in medical knowledge and clinical care. Recently the neonatal mortality rate has plateaued, but this may be due to increasing numbers babies who are born alive at very early gestations, who sadly have poorer outcomes.

Definitions

A stillborn baby is one who has died before or during birth, at or after 24 weeks of pregnancy.

A neonatal death happens in the first 28 days after birth.

Stillbirths and baby deaths that happen in the first seven days of life, are sometimes counted together and called perinatal deaths.

The above information is reprinted with kind permission from Sands (Stillbirth and Neonatal Death Charity).
© 2021 Sands (Stillbirth and Neonatal Death Charity)

www.sands.org.uk

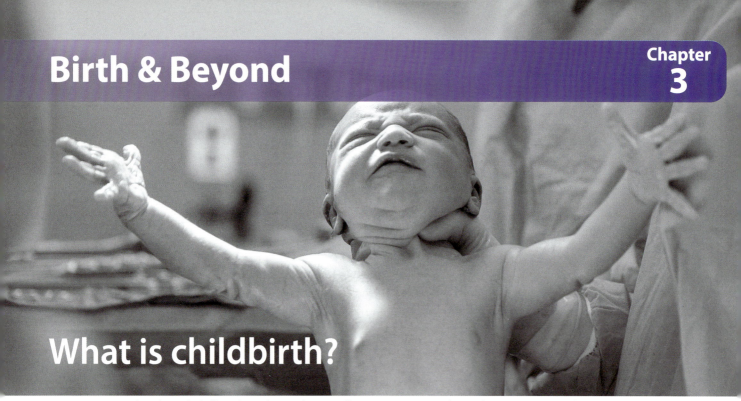

What is childbirth?

As a general rule, childbirth takes place after nine months of pregnancy, however, it can occur prematurely. Labour happens in three stages, but established labour is achieved when the cervix is dilated to 3cm. Childbirth is different for every mother and infant, with different delivery methods, positions and pain relief options available.

As childbirth can be painful, there are various options of pain relief to choose from:

♦ **Self-help:** by being more relaxed in labour it is likely to be less painful. Keeping moving, having a bath, having a massage and deep breathing can all help to relax you.

♦ **Gas and air:** a mixture of oxygen and nitrous oxide can make the pain of labour more manageable. It is given via a mask held by yourself.

♦ **Pethidine injections:** this is injected into your thigh or buttock and helps you to relax, lasting for up to four hours.

♦ **Epidural:** this is a form of local anaesthetic which numbs the nerves carrying pain signals from the birth canal to the brain. For many women, it can provide total pain relief. It is administered via a needle placed in your lower back.

The different methods of delivery include:

♦ **Natural birth** – this is a vaginal delivery without pain relief.

♦ **Vaginal birth with pain relief**

♦ **Water birth** – some women find that a birthing pool relaxes them and relieves their pain.

♦ **Caesarean section** – a surgical procedure in which the infant is delivered through an incision in the mother's abdomen and uterus. This might be necessary if the baby is too large, is in the wrong position or the baby is in distress, or if previous births have been done via caesarean.

What does childbirth consist of?

Labour usually begins with your amniotic sac rupturing. This is often called your 'water-breaking'. The fluid should be clear and odourless. You will start to have contractions following this. Contractions are the tightening and releasing of the muscles surrounding your uterus. They are meant to help push the baby during delivery through the cervix. It can feel like heavy menstrual cramping or pressure. If contractions are lasting for about a minute and are roughly five minutes apart, this is considered true labour and not Braxton-Hicks contractions which can begin as early as the second trimester.

First stage of labour:

This is the longest stage and starts with contractions which aim to dilate the cervix. This is called the latent phase and is when the cervix starts to soften ahead of the birth. This stage can take hours or even days. Established labour is when the cervix has dilated to at least 3cm. Once in established labour you might be offered pain relief and you will be monitored regularly. During this time your cervix will continue to dilate as it needs to be open about 10cm to enable the baby to pass through. This can take up to 12 hours in a first-time birth.

Second stage of labour:

This is when the cervix is fully dilated (10cm) until the actual birth of the baby. Before birthing commences you will need to find a comfortable position, for which there are several (standing, sitting, kneeling, squatting or lying on your side). Once fully dilated, you will feel an urge to push. When you are having contractions it can be helpful to push. This stage of labour can be the hardest and can last up to three hours.

Once the baby's head is almost ready to be delivered, you will stop pushing so that the head is birthed slowly, allowing the skin and muscles to stretch. Sometimes an episiotomy will be needed to avoid tearing and to speed up the birth. Once the head is delivered, the rest of the baby is birthed in the next few contractions. Once birthed, you can normally hold your baby immediately, skin-to-skin.

Third stage of labour:

This occurs after the baby is born and involves the delivery of the placenta. This may be done naturally, but sometimes it might require help from your doctor. The umbilical cord is usually cut between 1 and 5 minutes after birth.

Preparation for childbirth:

Many pregnant women attend childbirth preparation classes, where they explain what the stages of delivery are and how they can cope. Breathing and relaxation techniques are taught, as well as the first steps of care that their new-born should receive.

Aftercare:

After delivery, it is important that the mother rest as much as possible. You will suffer some blood loss, similar to the menstrual period, which will last a few weeks. Do not use tampons for this, but instead use absorbent sanitary pads. If you have had an episiotomy you will have some stitches which need to be kept clean. These are usually dissolvable, but sometimes do need to be removed.

The above information is reprinted with kind permission from Top Doctors.
© 2021 Top Doctors

www.topdoctors.co.uk

What are my options for giving birth?

You may be trying to decide whether to have a vaginal birth or a caesarean section (c-section). Speak to your midwife or doctor as soon as possible. They can give you the information and support you need to understand your birth options.

Can I choose what type of birth I want?

Yes, you can usually choose how and where you give birth.

The type of birth you have will depend on:

♦ your preferences

♦ your and your baby's health

♦ where you choose to give birth.

Speak to your midwife as early as you can about your options. They can explain the benefits and risks of vaginal and c-section births.

If you or your baby have any illnesses or complications, your midwife or doctor may offer you:

♦ an induction for early vaginal birth

♦ a planned c-section.

They will explain the advantages and disadvantages of both options.

You have the right to take part in discussions with your doctor or midwife to help you make informed decisions about your care. Doctors cannot give you treatment you do not want unless you're not able to give consent (permission), for example in an emergency.

Birthrights has more information about your rights during pregnancy and birth.

I want a vaginal birth but need a more specific plan

Speak to your midwife as soon as you can if you want a vaginal birth but you're feeling anxious or worried. You may be worried that you won't be able to cope or you may have had a difficult birth before. Your midwife will offer you support throughout your pregnancy and help you plan the birth.

Past trauma

Your past experiences may affect how you choose to give birth. For example, you may be worried about having a vaginal birth if you have a fear of childbirth or you have experienced sexual abuse.

Try to speak to your midwife or doctor early on in your pregnancy about your concerns. It's up to you how much you tell them about your past experiences.

They will help you plan what you would and would not like to happen during labour and the birth. For example, you may want to avoid vaginal examinations or you may want to visit the delivery room in advance.

Your midwife or doctor may refer you to a health professional who specialises in mental health. The specialist can offer you emotional support. Recording your wishes in a birth plan may help to reassure you about the birth.

Can I have a c-section if I don't have a medical reason?

A c-section is major abdominal surgery, which carries some risks for you and your baby. Speak to your midwife about any worries you have about giving birth. They may be able to reassure you or refer you for more support. You can ask your midwife to refer you to another health professional, such as:

♦ an obstetrician – a doctor who specialises in care during pregnancy, labour and after birth

♦ an anaesthetist – a doctor who gives pain relief and anaesthetic for medical operations and procedures

♦ a consultant midwife

B.R.A.I.N

is a quick and easy tool to use when making decisions about your care. It can help you to ask the relevant questions so that you can be well informed. All information should be shared with you in an evidence-based, non-judgemental, unbiased and empathetic manner.

B – Benefits
What are the benefits of having this procedure/intervention?

R – Risks
What are the risks of this process for me, my baby and how will it affect my labour and birth?

A – Alternatives
What are the alternatives to this procedure - can it be carried out differently or can a different process be used?

I – Instinct
What do you feel is right for you, what feels safest, what's your gut instinct?

N – Nothing
What happens if I do nothing, I'm not ready to decide yet? I dont want to do anything right now/I need time.

Source: Tommy's Pregnancy Hub

♦ a birth planning midwife

♦ a specialist mental health midwife.

Your midwife or doctor can tell you what a c-section involves and how it may affect you after the birth and in future pregnancies. Find out more about the benefits and risks of a c-section.

You can choose to have a c-section, after talking to your healthcare team about the benefits and risks. If you feel your obstetrician does not support your choice of birth, you can ask to see a different doctor.

Some hospitals cannot get funding for c-sections without a medical need. If this happens, you can ask to move to a hospital in a different area.

"I asked for a c-section because I had a difficult first birth followed by postnatal depression and post-traumatic stress. The team looking after me reassured me throughout my pregnancy but reminded me of my other birth options. They helped with my birth plan, which included different options, including a planned c-section, trying a vaginal birth and what would happen if I went into labour early. Having this reassurance reduced my anxiety and helped me feel confident about what I wanted for the birth."

Laura

16 July 2021

The above information is reprinted with kind permission from Tommy's © 2021 Tommy's

www.tommys.org

Your body after the birth

Advice about stitches, piles, bleeding and other physical changes after birth, plus tips to help you make a healthy recovery.

Stitches

If you've had stitches after tearing or an episiotomy (cut), bathe them every day to help prevent infection. Have a bath or shower with plain warm water then carefully pat yourself dry.

If your stitches are sore or uncomfortable, tell your midwife.

Painkillers can help. If you're breastfeeding, check with your pharmacist, midwife or GP before you buy over-the-counter painkillers.

Stitches usually dissolve by the time the cut or tear has healed, but sometimes they have to be taken out.

Going to the toilet

At first, the thought of peeing can be a bit frightening – because of the soreness. Drinking lots of water dilutes your urine, which may make it sting less.

Tell your midwife if:

♦ you're finding it really difficult to pee

♦ you feel very sore

♦ you notice an unpleasant smell

You probably won't have a poo for a few days after the birth, but it's important not to let yourself get constipated.

Eat plenty of fresh fruit, vegetables, salad, wholegrain cereals and wholemeal bread, and drink plenty of water.

If you've had stitches, it's very unlikely you'll break them, or open up the cut or tear again.

It might feel better if you hold a pad of clean tissue over the stitches when pooing. Try not to strain.

Talk to your midwife or GP if you have constipation that won't go away. A gentle laxative may help.

Also tell your midwife or GP if poo is leaking or you're pooing when you don't mean to.

Bladder control

After having a baby, it's quite common to leak a bit of pee if you laugh, cough or move suddenly.

Pelvic floor exercises can help with this but tell your GP at your postnatal check if they aren't. They may refer you to a physiotherapist.

Piles

Piles are very common after birth but usually disappear within a few days.

Eat plenty of fresh fruit, vegetables, salad, wholegrain cereals and wholemeal bread, and drink plenty of water. This should make pooing easier and less painful.

Try not to push or strain – this will make the piles worse.

Let your midwife know if you feel very uncomfortable. They can give you a cream to soothe the piles.

Bleeding after birth (lochia)

You'll bleed from your vagina after the birth. It will be quite heavy at first, and you'll need super-absorbent sanitary towels. Change them regularly, washing your hands before and afterwards.

It isn't a good idea to use tampons until after your 6-week postnatal check because they could increase your chance of getting an infection.

You may notice the bleeding is redder and heavier when you breastfeed. This happens because breastfeeding makes your womb contract. You may also feel cramps similar to period pains.

The bleeding will carry on for a few weeks. It will gradually turn a brownish colour and decrease until it finally stops.

If you're losing blood in large clots, tell your midwife. You may need some treatment.

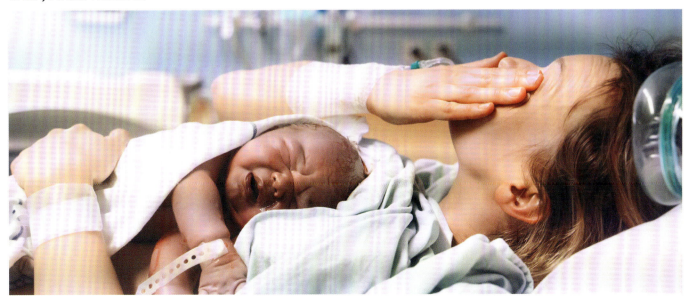

When will my periods start again after pregnancy?

It's hard to be exact about when your periods will start again, as everyone is different.

If you bottle feed your baby, or combine bottle feeding with breastfeeding, your first period could start as soon as 5 to 6 weeks after you give birth.

If you fully breastfeed (including at night) without any bottle feeding, your periods may not start again until you start to reduce breastfeeding.

How soon after giving birth can I get pregnant?

You can get pregnant as little as 3 weeks after the birth of your baby, even if you're breastfeeding and your periods have not started again yet.

How soon can I use tampons after giving birth?

You should not use tampons until you've had your 6-week postnatal check. This is because you'll still have a wound where the placenta joined with the wall of your womb, and you may also have tears or cuts in or around your vagina.

Using internal sanitary products like tampons and menstrual cups before this wound has healed could increase your chance of getting an infection.

Use maternity pads or sanitary towels during this time while your body is still healing.

Breasts

To begin with, your breasts will produce a yellowish liquid called colostrum for your baby.

On the third or fourth day, they may feel tight and tender as they start to produce milk.

Wearing a supportive nursing bra may help. Speak to your midwife if you're very uncomfortable.

Tummy

After delivery, your tummy will probably still be a lot bigger than before pregnancy. This is partly because your muscles have stretched.

If you eat a balanced diet and get some exercise, your shape should gradually return.

Breastfeeding helps because it makes your womb contract. You may feel quite painful period-like cramps while you're feeding.

15 April 2021

The above information is reprinted with kind permission from the NHS.
© Crown copyright 2021
This information is licensed under the Open Government Licence v3.0
To view this licence, visit http://www.nationalarchives.gov.uk/doc/open-government-licence/ **OGL**

www.nhs.uk

Recovery – Caesarean section

You'll probably be in hospital for 3 or 4 days after a caesarean section, and may need to take things easy for several weeks.

Recovering in hospital

The average stay in hospital after a caesarean is around 3 or 4 days.

You may be able to go home sooner than this if both you and your baby are well.

While in hospital:

♦ you'll be given painkillers to reduce any discomfort
♦ you'll have regular close contact with your baby and can start breastfeeding
♦ you'll be encouraged to get out of bed and move around as soon as possible
♦ you can eat and drink as soon as you feel hungry or thirsty
♦ a thin, flexible tube called a catheter will remain in your bladder for at least 12 hours
♦ your wound will be covered with a dressing for at least 24 hours

When you're well enough to go home, you'll need to arrange for someone to give you a lift as you will not be able to drive for a few weeks.

Looking after your wound

Your midwife should also advise you on how to look after your wound.

You'll usually be advised to:

♦ gently clean and dry the wound every day
♦ wear loose, comfortable clothes and cotton underwear
♦ take a painkiller if the wound is sore – for most women, it's better to take paracetamol or ibuprofen (but not aspirin) while you're breastfeeding
♦ watch out for signs of infection

Non-dissolvable stitches or staples will usually be taken out by your midwife after 5 to 7 days.

Your scar

The wound in your tummy will eventually form a scar.

This will usually be a horizontal scar about 10 to 20cm long, just below your bikini line.

In rare cases, you may have a vertical scar just below your bellybutton.

The scar will probably be red and obvious at first, but should fade with time and will often be hidden by your pubic hair.

On darker skin, the scar tissue may fade to leave a brown or white mark.

Controlling pain and bleeding

Most women experience some discomfort for the first few days after a caesarean, and for some women the pain can last several weeks.

You should be given regular painkillers to take at home for as long as you need them, such as paracetamol or ibuprofen.

Aspirin and the stronger painkiller codeine present in co-codamol is not usually recommended if you're breastfeeding.

Your doctor will be able to advise you on the most suitable painkiller for you to take.

You may also have some vaginal bleeding.

Use sanitary pads rather than tampons to reduce the risk of spreading infection into the vagina, and get medical advice if the bleeding is heavy.

Returning to your normal activities

Try to stay mobile and do gentle activities, such as going for a daily walk, while you're recovering to reduce the risk of blood clots. Be careful not to overexert yourself.

You should be able to hold and carry your baby once you get home.

But you may not be able to do some activities straight away, such as:

♦ driving
♦ exercising
♦ carrying anything heavier than your baby
♦ having sex

Only start to do these things again when you feel able to do so and do not find them uncomfortable. This may not be for 6 weeks or so.

Ask your midwife for advice if you're unsure when it's safe to start returning to your normal activities.

You can also ask a GP at your 6-week postnatal check.

When to get medical advice

Contact your midwife or a GP straight away if you have any of the following symptoms after a caesarean:

♦ severe pain
♦ leaking urine
♦ pain when peeing
♦ heavy vaginal bleeding
♦ your wound becomes more red, painful and swollen
♦ a discharge of pus or foul-smelling fluid from your wound
♦ a cough or shortness of breath
♦ swelling or pain in your lower leg

These symptoms may be the sign of an infection or blood clot, which should be treated as soon as possible.

27 June 2019

The above information is reprinted with kind permission from the NHS.
© Crown copyright 2021
This information is licensed under the Open Government Licence v3.0
To view this licence, visit http://www.nationalarchives.gov.uk/doc/open-government-licence/ **OGL**

www.nhs.uk

Tokophobia is an extreme fear of childbirth. Here's how to recognise and treat it

An article from The Conversation.

By Julie Jomeen, Professor of Midwifery and Dean in the Faculty of Health Sciences, Southern Cross University, Catriona Jones, Senior Research Fellow in Maternal and Reproductive Health, University of Hull, Claire Marshall, National Institute for Health Research Fellow, University of Hull, Colin Martin, Adjunct professor, Southern Cross University

Many pregnant women worry about birth. Some, however, suffer from a much more serious condition called tokophobia: a severe and unreasoning dread of childbirth, which is sometimes accompanied by a disgust of pregnancy.

At its most extreme, tokophobia can lead to:

- an obsessive use of contraception to prevent pregnancy
- termination of pregnancy
- not attending maternity care appointments
- post-traumatic stress disorder and/or other mental health disorders and mother-baby bonding difficulties.

Tokophobia comes in two forms: primary (in women who have not had a baby before) and secondary (women who have previously had a baby). Women with tokophobia in a previous pregnancy are more likely to have it in a subsequent pregnancy, resulting in a potential cycle of anxiety and depression.

Our new paper, published in the *Journal of Reproductive and Infant Psychology*, reflects on a recent meeting of researchers and clinicians about what's missing from the way we identify and treat tokophobia.

Hard to define, hard to screen for

It's hard to say how many women are affected by tokophobia; it's been defined and measured using different questionnaires. One research paper estimated the prevalence of tokophobia at 14% of pregnant women worldwide.

Screening for tokophobia is not common practice around the world. Screening questionnaires sometimes ask the woman questions about her mood, whether she has fears for herself or her baby, about feeling so afraid of childbirth she's considered terminating the pregnancy, or feeling fear so overwhelming it interferes with eating, work or sleep.

In other words, tokophobia goes beyond normal childbirth concerns and worries, and becomes an intense and irrational fear of pregnancy and/or labour.

It's important women with this condition are identified as soon as possible but that often only happens when they seek specialised professional help. This can sometimes (but not always) take the form of a request for a termination of pregnancy or caesarean section.

Treatment options

Treatment for tokophobia remains patchy but should be determined based on factors such as the woman's level of fear, stage of pregnancy and her individual wishes.

Early conversations about fear of childbirth — and understanding exactly what those fears are — may reduce negative impact and prevent anxiety.

For women with birth trauma (and potential secondary tokophobia), helping them prepare for uncertainty and building trust in themselves and their caregivers can result in a future positive experience.

Approaches that may help include:

- additional midwifery support to discuss the birth, with continuity of care, which is where the same midwife and/or midwifery care team sees the woman throughout pregnancy and labour
- involvement of the obstetrician in decision-making around birth
- extra education about childbirth
- the involvement of the birth partner
- supported visits to the delivery suite, and
- the development of a supportive birth plan.

Pathways of care

The way childbirth is often depicted in the media may play a role in setting birth up in women's minds as a negative experience. But it's important women share birth stories - the good and the bad. Like-minded peer support mechanisms, including parenting forums, which can be really helpful for some women.

During pregnancy, women should be encouraged to share their fears with their maternity care provider and ask questions.

Our understanding of fear of childbirth has undoubtedly increased, and some pioneering "pathways of care" for women with tokophobia already exist.

But there is much work left to do if we are to understand and identify when standard worries deviate from expected levels to problematic levels.

We owe it to women and babies everywhere to find better ways to support women with tokophobia and maximise their chances of a positive birth experience.

3 December 2020

The above information is reprinted with kind permission from The Conversation.
© 2010-2021, The Conversation Trust (UK) Limited

www.theconversation.com

What you should know about psychological birth trauma

Thousands of UK mums experience birth trauma every year – but we don't talk much about the psychological effects.

By Tanyel Mustafa

So charities and organisations are coming together to change that with Birth Trauma Awareness Week, which runs until July 25.

Midwife Marley, who works with breastfeeding brand Lansinoh, says: 'Psychological birth trauma is distress experienced by a mother during or after childbirth.

'It often occurs as a result of a physically traumatic birth but not always. It can also refer to how a woman is left feeling after her birth and often the effects of birth trauma can emerge and continue for some time after the baby is born.

'Some people describe feeling fearful, helpless or unheard during their birth experience. Shock, panic, guilt or emotional numbness are other words that have been used to describe how they felt. Birth trauma can lead to panic attacks.'

Lesley Gilchrist, a registered midwife and co-founder of My Expert Midwife, explains that in some cases, it can be so severe, it becomes post traumatic stress disorder (PTSD).

Though PTSD was formerly known as shellshock and linked to WW1 soldiers, it's a very real possibility that new mums can experience this after a traumatic birth.

Although it's currently unresearched, a 2017 study estimates that 4% of births lead to PTSD, which can last weeks, months or even years.

'It has not been until relatively recently that PTSD has been recognised as a condition suffered by many after childbirth, with research estimating as many as 30,000 sufferers from birth trauma every year in the UK,' Lesley tells us.

Some symptoms may be similar to postnatal depression (PND) but Marley says PND can occur regardless of whether a birth is traumatic or not and the two conditions should not be confused.

So what does birth trauma look like?

Experiences of birth trauma will differ from person to person, but there are some common themes.

Lesley explains: 'It can cause flashbacks, nightmares and guilt about not enjoying parenthood. Other symptoms include feelings of panic and being hypervigilant over baby.

'You are more likely to be affected by birth trauma if your birth didn't go as you imagined, or if you experienced procedures which frightened you during your labour, birth or in the immediate postnatal period.'

The causes can be vast, but Lesley says the following are common:

- Having an assisted delivery using forceps or ventouse
- Having medical interventions that you didn't think you would need
- Going to the operating theatre for an emergency caesarean section
- Having an ineffective epidural or being unable to access an epidural or pain relief when you felt that you needed it
- A lack of privacy and dignity during care procedures. These include simple things such as people talking behind curtains about your care and not involving you
- Feeling like events have overtaken your control
- You or your baby were sick or ill during or after the birth and you feared for yours or their life

Dealing with birth trauma, can be 'debilitating', Lesley adds.

She says: 'It can prevent you from enjoying parenthood and family life and affect how you feel about your baby and future pregnancies.'

If you are struggling, Lesley advises contacting the hospital where you received care during the pregnancy to request a debrief to help you get a better understanding of what happened.

'This is an appointment for you to sit with a midwife or doctor and go through your notes to examine the events which caused your trauma,' she says.

'Equally, you may feel as though you want further investigations surrounding what happened. This can be done by contacting your hospital's Patient Advice and Liaison Service (PALS).'

Counselling and therapy can be offered too by a GP, as this mental health condition shouldn't be brushed off.

Due to our cultural shyness and even shame around mental health issues, it's important to recognise that birth trauma is a real condition – that sense of shame could be the very thing that stops someone from seeking help.

20 July 2021

The above information is reprinted with kind permission from *Metro* & DMG Media Licensing.
© 2021 Associated Newspapers Limited

www.metro.co.uk

Postnatal depression (PND)

Postnatal/postpartum depression (PND) is not the same as the 'baby blues'. It is a mental health condition that needs treatment, so it's important to ask for help.

What is the difference between postnatal depression and the baby blues?

Having the 'baby blues' after giving birth is very common. It usually starts in the week after you've given birth and stops by the time your baby is around ten days old.

Symptoms of 'baby blues' can include:

♦ feeling emotional and irrational

♦ bursting into tears for no apparent reason

♦ feeling irritable or touchy

♦ feeling depressed or anxious.

These are all normal feelings caused by hormone changes as your body gets used to not being pregnant anymore. You don't need any treatment for the baby blues, but it can be helpful to talk to someone about how you're feeling.

Postnatal depression is when you have feelings of sadness, hopelessness, guilt or self-blame all the time for weeks or months after you've had a baby. Some women have depression when they are pregnant. This is called antenatal depression.

The symptoms can vary from mild to severe and it can affect women in different ways. Some women may find it difficult to look after themselves and their baby if they have severe depression.

Depression is a mental health condition. It is not a sign of weakness, something that will go away on its own or that you should just 'snap out of.' The good news is that postnatal depression can be treated with the right care and support and most women will make a full recovery.

It's important to ask for help if you think you are depressed.

'It was a difficult birth and although I loved her because she was my child, I felt there was something missing. There's so much pressure and expectation on new mothers - and I wondered what was wrong with me.' - Caroline, mum of one

What are the symptoms of postnatal depression?

You may have postnatal depression if you have:

♦ feeling of sadness and low mood that won't go away

♦ lost interest in life and you're not enjoying the things you used to

♦ problems sleeping, such as having trouble getting back to sleep after caring for your baby at night, even when the baby is asleep and you're feeling exhausted

♦ difficulty concentrating and making decisions

♦ low self-confidence

♦ poor appetite (not eating enough)

♦ feeling very agitated or, alternatively, you can't be bothered with anything (apathy)

♦ feelings of guilt and self-blame

♦ thinking about, and even planning, suicide.

You may not have all these symptoms and they may come on gradually or you may suddenly start to feel very low.

If you're feeling like you want to die, it's important to tell someone. This could be a family member, friend, your GP or midwife. You can also call the Samaritans on 116 123.

'I came home on day three or four and the moment I walked into the house I burst into tears. I got the same anxiety feeling, the feeling I wasn't going to be able to cope with this.' – Stephanie, mum of two

Trust yourself. You are the best judge of whether your feelings are normal for you. Talk to your midwife or GP if you think you have any symptoms of depression and they last for more than two weeks.

How common is it?

Very common. More than 1 in every 10 new mothers experience postnatal depression within a year of giving birth. New fathers can get postnatal depression, too.

What causes depression?

You may be more likely to get postnatal depression if you have:

♦ had mental health problems before, particularly depression

♦ had mental health problems during your pregnancy

♦ no close friends or family to support you

♦ a poor relationship with your partner

♦ had a lot of stress in your life recently, such as a bereavement

♦ had the baby blues.

You may not relate to anything on this list. But having a baby is a life changing event, which can be stressful and exhausting. This alone is enough to cause depression.

What should I do?

Tell your midwife, health visitor or doctor how you feel. Some women feel very distressed or guilty at feeling low at a time when everyone expects them to be happy. Remember that healthcare professionals won't judge you. They understand that depression is a mental health condition. It is not your fault, or something that you just need to 'get over' or move on from. They will focus on helping you find the right treatment and support so you can take care of yourself and your baby.

If you find it difficult to talk about your thoughts and feelings, you could write down what you want to say first, or you may want to have someone with you. The important thing is to let someone know so that you can get the right help as soon as possible.

'I knew something wasn't right but I didn't want to admit it. I thought I would be a failure if I admitted that I was struggling with being a mum. One day I went out for a walk and nearly didn't go home. I thought my husband and son would be better off without me. I knew then it was time to ask for help' – Ruth

What is the treatment for depression?

The good news is that postnatal depression can be treated - it is a temporary illness that you can recover from. The treatment is likely to depend on how severe your depression is.

'It's difficult trying to find out what's wrong with you. Is it just being a new mum? Is it you're anxious because you can't settle the baby? Is it postnatal depression? There are so many things that overlap.' – Emily, mum of one

If you have mild depression, the doctor may recommend an exercise programme and/or guided self-help. If you live in England you can self refer for talking therapy or self help. You may be offered medication, especially if you have had depression before or the depression is severe.

If you have mild to moderate depression and have had no previous depression, you may be offered guided self-help or a 'talking treatment' (psychological therapy), such as counselling. Your doctor will discuss the options with you, depending on what is appropriate for you and your symptoms.

If you have severe depression or moderate depression and had previous depression your doctor might recommend counselling and antidepressants.

If you are planning to breast-feed your baby, talk to the doctor about this so that they can factor this into the treatment discussions. Some antidepressants are not recommended for breastfeeding and the doctor who is treating you will prescribe one that is suitable instead.

'I was on medication...and I was under close review because things were bad... But by about four months things started to lift. I've always described it like layers of cling-film coming off.' – Stephanie, mum of two

How can I help myself?

There's no evidence that there's anything you can do to prevent getting depression. But there are a few things you can do to make things easier for yourself.

It's important to tell the midwife or doctor if you have had depression in the past because you may be more likely to get depression in this pregnancy or after you give birth. They can then give you the best support to reduce the chances of you getting depression again.

It also helps to know what the symptoms of postnatal depression are so you can ask for help if you get them.

Depression can make you want to hide away from the world and you may feel like you don't want to do anything at all. But it is important to take care of yourself. Start with little activities, take things at your own pace and most importantly, ask for help if you need it. Here are a few ideas.

♦ Talk to someone you trust about your feelings, such as your partner, family or a friend.

♦ Try not to feel guilty, ashamed or embarrassed. These feelings are not your fault.

♦ Try some of our top tips for looking after your emotional wellbeing.

♦ Get some exercise every day – keeping active will release some feel-good endorphins.

♦ Eat well even if you don't have much appetite.

♦ Avoid alcohol and smoking – they can harm your baby and make you feel worse.

♦ Read about planning ahead for emotional wellbeing for after birth

♦ Use the Tommy's Wellbeing Plan to think about how much support you will need.

'It was really only a week after she was born and things started to go right downhill again. I just couldn't get up. I couldn't get out of bed. It wasn't even about bonding with her. I just didn't want to exist anymore.' – Abby, mum of one

More information and support

♦ PANDAS provides telephone support, online information and local support groups for pregnancy depression and postnatal depression.

♦ APNI (Association for Postnatal Illness) provides telephone support and online information on postnatal depression.

♦ MIND is a mental health charity providing information, support, local groups and an online chatroom.

♦ Local support groups may also be available. Check out what's on offer at Netmums or ask your GP. You can also chat to other new mums suffering from the baby blues, PND, PTSD and more in BabyCentre's friendly support group.

19 October 2018

The above information is reprinted with kind permission from Tommy's.
© 2021 Tommy's

www.tommys.org

The benefits of breastfeeding for parents and baby

Breastmilk is the best form of nutrition for your baby. It provides the nutrients your baby needs to grow and develop and helps the child to fight infections during infancy. It also has benefits for those who are breastfeeding. Yet, some people are unable to breastfeed, and others may choose not to. There are good alternatives to breastfeeding, such as formula feeding or mixed feeding. This article provides an overview of the benefits of breastfeeding and information about alternative feeding methods.

What are the health benefits for the baby?

Breastfeeding is recommended around the world as the best source of nutrition and hydration for babies. In addition, breastfeeding protects babies against certain infections and other conditions in early childhood. Any amount of breastmilk is protective, but the longer you breastfeed the greater the benefits.

Babies who are breastfed exclusively for at least 6 months are less likely to develop:

- Gastrointestinal infections (diarrhoea and vomiting)
- Ear infections and respiratory infections
- Inflammatory bowel diseases
- Sudden infant death syndrome (SIDS)
- Asthma and wheezing
- Childhood leukaemia.

Breastmilk is made up of almost 90% water, along with the fats, proteins, carbohydrates and micronutrients babies need to grow. It also contains other components, such as antibodies, antioxidants, growth factors, and hormones. Antibodies and other immune molecules in breastmilk are believed to play an essential role in the protection of babies from infections.

When you are exposed to any bacteria or virus, your body produces antibodies to fight it off. When breastfeeding, these antibodies will be passed on through breastmilk and will protect the baby against infections and illnesses. When a baby does get sick, they frequently pass on germs to their parents, causing their immune system to respond and make antibodies. These antibodies can be passed on to the baby through breastfeeding, to support the baby in fighting their infection.

Research has shown some additional potential long-term benefits of breastfeeding, including a lower risk of developing diabetes and obesity in adulthood. The bacteria in breast milk may also further enhance the baby's health by preventing disease-causing microorganisms to grow and promoting growth of beneficial microbes in the gut.

What are the health benefits for the breastfeeding mother?

Breastfeeding also has some health benefits for the breastfeeding mother. In the short term, breastfeeding helps support quicker recovery after delivery. The hormone oxytocin, which is produced during breastfeeding, causes the uterus to contract, bringing it back to its original size, and reduces the amount of bleeding after birth.

Breastfeeding may also lower the risk of developing breast and ovarian cancer, type 2 diabetes and high blood pressure of those breastfeeding.

How long should I breastfeed?

The World Health Organization (WHO) recommends exclusive breastfeeding for at least 6 months. 'Exclusive' means only feeding breastmilk, no water or any other fluids or solids. It is usually recommended to introduce complementary (solid) foods at 6 months of age, alongside continued breastfeeding for up to 2 years or for as long as both you and your baby enjoy it. Even if you breastfeed for a shorter period than the recommended 6 months, it is more beneficial than not breastfeeding at all.

Some scientific research indicates that introducing foods alongside breastfeeding between 4 and 6 months of age is helpful in the prevention and management of food sensitivities and allergies. This is why certain national guidelines already advise to introduce mixtures of fruits and vegetables, and small amounts of common allergens such as egg and peanut, from 4 months of age and onwards (e.g. Belgium and the Netherlands). It is also important to introduce each new food one at a time, to more easily identify potential intolerances or allergies.

What if I cannot breastfeed?

Breastfeeding may be challenging and can be stressful and painful. Problems such as low milk supply, sore and cracked nipples, breast engorgement or breast infection,

Options if you can't or don't choose to breastfeed

formula milk

pumping or expressing breastmilk

human milk from accredited milk banks or hospitals

Source: Eufic

may affect breastfeeding. Some babies have difficulties with latching on properly or suckling effectively. Combining breastfeeding with returning to work can also be a major challenge. Occasionally, mothers are unable to breastfeed as their bodies do not produce any or too little milk for the new-born baby.

If you are struggling to breastfeed, your doctor, midwife or a lactation specialist can offer support and guidance to help you towards a positive breastfeeding experience.

If you cannot, or choose not to, breastfeed, there are several good and healthy alternatives, including formula feeding or exclusive pumping. Some people prefer the flexibility of mixed feeding, which is a combination of feeding breast milk and formula. It is good to be aware of the differences between breastfeeding and formula feeding before making a decision that is right for you.

Pumping or expressing breastmilk and feeding your baby with a bottle is a good way to still offer the baby the benefits of breastmilk if exclusive breastfeeding is not possible or desired. Many breastfeeding mothers start pumping breastmilk when they go back to work or if they experience problems with breastfeeding. Some breastfeeding mothers express their milk by hand, while others use a pump. The baby can receive exclusively expressed milk, or this can be combined with breastfeeding and/or formula feeding. However, be mindful of safe storage and reheating of expressed milk. Expressed milk can be kept refrigerated (at 4°C or lower) and used within 3-4 days, or it can be safely frozen for up to 6 months.

If someone has problems breastfeeding, one alternative is to provide the baby with milk donated by someone else, however this is usually a short-term solution carried out in hospital settings. Donated breast milk is available at human milk banks. Donated milk should be properly screened to ensure the milk is safe and should only be obtained through official milk banks. It can also be difficult to obtain the quantity of milk that you need to feed a baby exclusively on donated milk. Please consult your doctor before deciding to feed your baby donated milk.

Is breastfeeding in public legal?

Some people might feel uncomfortable around breastfeeding in public. However, breastfeeding in public, for example in parks, restaurants, and public transport, is legally protected in most European countries.

Making the right choice for you and your baby

In most cases, breastmilk is the recommended option for babies, due to the health benefits described in this article. Although breastfeeding can be challenging during the first weeks after delivery, it can also be a wonderful experience for both the breastfeeding mother and the baby. Remember that your doctor, midwife or a lactation specialist are there to support the process of learning to breastfeed. Ultimately, only you can know what works best for you and your baby and, if needed, there are safe and healthy alternatives like expressed milk and formula.

1 August 2021

The above information is reprinted with kind permission from EUFIC.
© 2021 EUFIC

www.eufic.org

♦ 90 per cent of women get stretch marks when pregnant. (page 2)

♦ An odd, unpleasant or metallic taste in the mouth is quite a common symptom pregnant women experience. (page 6)

♦ There is no safe level of alcohol to drink when you are pregnant and the more you drink the greater the risk of harm to your baby. (page 10)

♦ Current health guidelines recommend that you limit your caffeine intake during pregnancy to 200mg a day. (page 10)

♦ Smoking during pregnancy can cause serious health problems for you and your baby. (page 10)

♦ Energy needs increase throughout pregnancy, but it is a myth that you need to "eat for two". (page 11)

♦ Undercooked or raw meats, including raw cured meats like salami, chorizo and Parma ham, can contain harmful parasites like Toxoplasma gondii or bacteria like Salmonella or Listeria. (page 14)

♦ If you are overweight you have an increased risk of problems during pregnancy. (page 17)

♦ Around 60,000 babies are born prematurely each year in the UK. (page 19)

♦ An estimated 1 in 5 pregnancies ended in miscarriage. (page 19)

♦ The NHS estimates that up to two thirds of early miscarriages are related to chromosome abnormalities. (page 20)

♦ Approximately 1-5% of all pregnancies will result in a missed miscarriage. (page 21)

♦ Each year in the UK nearly 12,000 women have ectopic pregnancies diagnosed. (page 22)

♦ Ectopic pregnancy is a common, occasionally life-threatening condition that affects 1 in 80 pregnancies. (page 23)

♦ Very rarely a pregnancy test can give a falsely negative result. (page 23)

♦ Miscarriage can happen any time between 12 and 24 weeks. (page 24)

♦ A 'missed' or 'silent miscarriage' occurs when the baby has died but the pregnancy hormones are still ongoing. (page 25)

♦ According to baby charity Tommy's, medical management is a successful method in 85 per cent of cases of missed miscarriage. (page 25)

♦ In 2017, one in every 238 births in the UK was a stillbirth. This equates to nine stillborn babies a day and around 3,200 stillbirths that year. (page 25)

♦ Every day in the UK around 14 babies die before, during or soon after birth. (page 27)

♦ ONS stats have confirmed that stillbirth rates are highest for Black women and higher for South Asian and Asian women and for those who live in deprived areas. (page 27)

♦ Around 100 babies die every year because of a trauma or event during birth that was not anticipated or well managed. (page 27)

♦ After having a baby, it's quite common to leak a bit of pee if you laugh, cough or move suddenly. (page 31)

♦ You can get pregnant as little as 3 weeks after the birth of your baby, even if you're breastfeeding and your periods have not started again yet. (page 32)

♦ As many as 30,000 mums suffer from birth trauma every year in the UK. (page 35)

♦ More than 1 in every 10 new mothers experience postnatal depression within a year of giving birth. (page 36)

♦ Breastmilk is made up of almost 90% water, along with the fats, proteins, carbohydrates and micronutrients babies need to grow. (page 38)

♦ The World Health Organization (WHO) recommends exclusive breastfeeding for at least 6 months. (page 38)

♦ Pumping or expressing breastmilk and feeding your baby with a bottle is a good way to still offer the baby the benefits of breastmilk if exclusive breastfeeding is not possible or desired. (page 39)

♦ Occasionally, mothers are unable to breastfeed as their bodies do not produce any or too little milk for the new-born baby. (page 39)

Birth rate

The number of live births within a population over a given period of time, often expressed as the number of births per 1,000 of the population.

Conception

The act of fertilisation, where an egg (ovum) joins together with a sperm (spermatozoon) to form an embryo or zygote. This term describes the moment a woman becomes pregnant.

Contraception

Anything which prevents conception, or pregnancy, from taking place. 'Barrier methods', such as condoms, work by stopping sperm from reaching an egg during intercourse and are also effective in preventing sexually transmitted infections (STI's). Hormonal methods such as the contraceptive pill change the way a woman's body works to prevent an egg from being fertilised. Emergency contraception, commonly known as the 'morning-after pill', is used after unprotected sex to prevent a fertilised egg from becoming implanted in the womb.

Ectopic pregnancy

An ectopic pregnancy is when a fertilised egg implants itself outside of the womb, usually in one of the fallopian tubes. The egg won't develop into a baby and can put the mother's life at risk if the pregnancy continues.

Embryo (zygote)

Between day 14 and week eight of pregnancy the fertilised egg is referred to as an embryo. A zygote is simply the scientific term for the fertilised egg which is made by the joining of an egg (ovum) and sperm (spermatozoon). After the eighth week of pregnancy an unborn baby is referred to as a foetus.

Foetal abnormality

An abnormal or disformed foetus. With unborn babies or foetuses this can refer to a disability or feature which would prevent a child from leading a relatively normal and happy life once it was born, and can, therefore, be a reason to terminate a pregnancy.

Foetus/Fetus

The unborn offspring of an animal or human being that has developed from an embryo.

Genes

A gene is an instruction and each of our cells contains tens of thousands of these instructions. In humans, these instructions work together to determine everything from our eye colour to our risk of heart disease. The reason we all have slightly different characteristics is that before we are born our parents' genes get shuffled about at random. The same principles apply to other animals and plants.

Genetic testing

This refers to a technique called pre-implantation genetic diagnosis (PGD). This allows parents to test for serious genetically inherited conditions such Huntington's disease or cystic fibrosis. There is a fear that genetic testing will be misused. However, it can be legally carried out if it is in the best interest for the embryo.

Gestation

The development period of an embryo or foetus between conception and birth. As the exact date of conception in humans can be difficult to identify it is usually dated from the beginning of a woman's previous menstrual period.

Infant mortality rate

The number of infant deaths (infants are usually defined as one year old or younger) per 1,000 live births of the population.

IVF (In vitro fertilisation)

IVF literally means 'fertilisation in glass', giving us the familiar term 'test tube baby'. IVF treatment is considered by couples who are having fertility problems and are not getting pregnant. Eggs are removed from the ovaries and fertilised with sperm in a laboratory dish before being placed in the woman's womb (a technique where the egg is fertilised by sperm outside of the body).

Maternity leave

Female employees have the statutory right to a minimum amount of time off during and following a pregnancy. Statutory maternity leave is currently 39 weeks paid, six weeks at 90% of full pay and the remainder at a flat rate (as of 2009 = £123.06), or 90% of your salary if that is less than the flat rate.

Miscarriage

A miscarriage is the loss of a baby before 24 weeks.

Neonatal

Referring to a newborn baby, specifically the first 28 days after birth.

Obstetricians and gynaecologists

A gynaecologist is a doctor who specialises in the health of the female reproductive system. An obstetrician is a doctor who specializes in pregnancy, childbirth, and a woman's reproductive system

Perinatal

Perinatal is the period of time when you become pregnant and up to a year after giving birth.

Pica

A disorder that involves the consumption of non-nutritive substances such as dirt, hair or sand.

Stillbirth

A stillbirth is when, unfortunately, the baby dies in the uterus after 24 weeks.

Activities

Brainstorming

♦   What do you know about pregnancy? Create a mindmap of the things that you know.

Research

♦   Do some research on the trimesters of pregnancy. Present your findings in an infographic.

♦   Do some research on 'pica', what sort of things may women crave in pregnancy and why?

♦   In small groups, do some research on mental health in pregnancy. Present your findings to the rest of the class.

♦   Do some research into charities and organisations that help people with pregnancy and issues with pregnancy and create a sign-posting poster with some information and contact details for those organisations.

♦   In pairs, do some research on foods to be avoided in pregnancy. Create a poster with some of these and what risks they carry for pregnant women and their babies.

♦   Have a look at the guidance on breastfeeding from the World Health Organization (WHO). Do you think that this is possible for all babies and mothers? Explain your reasons in a short report.

Design

♦   Look at one of the illustrations in this book, with a partner, discuss what you think the artist was trying to portray?

♦   Choose an article in this book and create your own illustration.

♦   Create a leaflet on healthy eating in pregnancy - use the articles in this book to help you.

♦   Design a poster to promote having a healthy pregnancy.

♦   Create a leaflet on recognising the signs of pre- or post-natal depression.

♦   Design a poster on the different options for feeding a baby.

♦   Design a leaflet on the things to avoid whilst pregnant.

Oral

♦   In small groups, discuss what you know about post-natal depression. Would you know how to spot the signs?

♦   In pairs, put together a healthy eating plan for a pregnant woman, using the articles in this book for guidance.

♦   As a class, discuss the things that should be avoided in pregnancy and why. Consider how to have a healthy pregnancy.

♦   As a class, discuss ways of feeding a baby. The World Health Organization (WHO) recommend exclusive breastfeeding for the first six months of a baby's life. Consider all options and why they may/may not be possible.

Reading/writing

♦   Choose one of the articles in this book and write a one paragraph summary. List three key points.

♦   Imagine that you are an agony aunt/uncle - write a letter from someone who is experiencing depression or anxiety about giving birth, or after the baby has arrived. Write a reply to them and give them some advice.

♦   Write a blog on what people can do to have a healthy pregnancy. Include three things that are beneficial to mother and baby.

♦   Imagine that you have tokophobia and write a diary entry about how you feel and any worries you might have.

♦   In pairs, discuss and list the things that someone may include on their birthplan.

Acknowledgements

The publisher is grateful for permission to reproduce the material in this book. While every care has been taken to trace and acknowledge copyright, the publisher tenders its apology for any accidental infringement or where copyright has proved untraceable. The publisher would be pleased to come to a suitable arrangement in any such case with the rightful owner.

The material reproduced in ISSUES books is provided as an educational resource only. The views, opinions and information contained within reprinted material in ISSUES books do not necessarily represent those of Independence Educational Publishers and its employees.

Images

Cover image courtesy of iStock. All other images courtesy of Freepix, Pixabay and Unsplash.

Illustrations

Simon Kneebone: pages 8, 30 & 39. Angelo Madrid: pages 3, 18 & 32.

Additional acknowledgements

With thanks to the Independence team: Shelley Baldry, Danielle Lobban and Jackie Staines.

Tracy Biram

Cambridge, September 2021